Introduction to the Internet for Engineers and Computer Scientists

Prentice Hall Modular Series for Engineering

Now, you can tailor your course materials to satisfy the needs of you and your students. With the Prentice Hall Modular Series for Engineering, you can mix and match these concise, inexpensive books for your classes. They are ideal for courses in which a variety of languages and software are being covered. All books focus on using real-world applications to help motivate your course.

Current Modules Include:

Introduction to MATLAB for Engineers and Scientists
Delores Etter – University of Colorado, Boulder
1996, 145 pp. 0-13-519703-1

Introduction to C++ for Engineers and Scientists
Delores Etter – University of Colorado, Boulder
1997, 160 pp. 0-13-254731-7

Introduction to ANSI C for Engineers and Scientists
Delores Etter – University of Colorado, Boulder
1996, 164 pp. 0-13-241381-7

Introduction to Fortran 90 for Engineers and Scientists
Larry Nyhoff and Sanford Leestma – both of Calvin College
1997, 336 pp. 0-13-505215-7

Fundamentals of AutoCAD
Mark Dix and Paul Riley – CAD Support Associates
1998, 250 pp. 0-13-860362-6

Engineering Design: A Day in the Life of Four Engineers
Mark Horenstein – Boston University
1998, 150 pp. 0-13-8660242-8

Introduction to the Internet for Engineers and Scientists
Scott James – GMI Institute
1998, 150 pp. 0-13-856691-7

Introduction to ProENGINEER
Jeffrey Freeman and Andrew Whelan – both of the University of Iowa
1998, 150 pp. 0-13-861048-7

Future Modules Include:

Engineering Ethics
Engineering Problem-Solving
Introduction to MS Word
Introduction to WordPerfect
Introduction to Excel
Introduction to Lotus 1-2-3

Introduction to the Internet for Engineers and Computer Scientists

SCOTT D. JAMES

Industrial & Manufacturing Systems Engineering Department
GMI Engineering & Management Institute

Prentice Hall
Upper Saddle River, New Jersey 07458

Library of Congress Cataloging-in-Publication Data

James, Scott D.,
Introduction to the Internet for engineers and computer scientists / Scott D. James.
p. cm. — (Prentice Hall modular series for engineering)
Includes bibliographical references and index.
ISBN 0-13-856691-7
1. Engineering—Computer network resources. 2. Internet (Computer network) 3. Computer science—Computer network resources.
I. Title. II. Series.
TA158.7.J36 1998
004.67'8'02462—dc21

97-17163
CIP

Editor-in-chief: **Marcia Horton**
Acquisitions editor: **Eric Svendsen**
Director of production and manufacturing: **David W. Riccardi**
Managing editor: **Bayani Mendoza DeLeon**
Production editor: **Judy Winthrop**
Cover director: **Jayne Conte**
Manufacturing buyer: **Julia Meehan**
Editorial assistant: **Andreau Au**

Printed in the United States of America

10 9 8 7 6 5 4 3 2 1

ISBN 0-13-856691-7

Prentice-Hall International (UK) Limited, *London*
Prentice-Hall of Australia Pty. Limited, *Sydney*
Prentice-Hall Canada, Inc., *Toronto*
Prentice-Hall Hispanoamericana, S.A., *Mexico*
Prentice-Hall of India Private Limited, *New Delhi*
Prentice-Hall of Japan, Inc., *Tokyo*
Simon & Schuster Asia Pte., Ltd., *Singapore*
Editora Prentice-Hall do Brazil, Ltda., *Rio de Janeiro*

DEDICATION:

This book is for Zard, Ash-Man, C-Meister & Oogie.
Thanks for the encouragement, support and time to work on this project!

Contents

Preface

The Internet is one of the fastest growing facets of the computer industry. The importance of this one area to engineers and scientists is paramount, and therefore, it is necessary for these individuals to learn what services the Internet offers and how to effectively utilize these services. Having access to timely data, keeping in contact with colleagues and the ability to use specific types of software are some of the key reasons for using the Internet, and these are the issues which this book will address.

PREREQUISITES

No prior experience with the Internet is assumed. However a decent working knowledge of a computer system is expected.

SCIENCE/ENGINEERING SPOTLIGHT

Each chapter is prefaced with a spotlight on some area in which science and/or engineering has been applied to help solve problems of current concern.

PRACTICE AND END OF CHAPTER PROBLEMS

Each chapter in the book includes two different content areas to allow the practice of the material which is presented. **Practice** problems are short-answer questions that usually follow each section to allow students to determine whether or not they have mastered the material which was just encountered.

At the end of each chapter, there is a set of **end-of-chapter problems** that increase in difficulty in order to examine the depth and application of the knowledge that the student has acquired.

NOTE TO THE INSTRUCTOR

This text has tried to stay software-independent in terms of demonstrating the different Internet tools. Rather than try to be an all-inclusive volume covering every major package that is used, this book discusses a concept and then tries to provide a quick example of using that particular tool or resource. This allows the course instructor to teach his or her students with whatever software the school provides. The book then becomes much more portable (and hopefully more usable) to both faculty and students.

ACKNOWLEDGEMENTS

I would like to express appreciation to a few folks who were key in the development of this text. First off, I would like to thank Eric Svensen, who convinced me to convert my own Internet class notes into a full blown text. I would also like to recognize Eric's assistant, Andrea Au, for putting up with my phone calls and questions.

I would also like to recognize the contributions of my students and peers who helped critique the original class notes and provided important feedback to bring the notes to their current state, and consequently this text into being.

Scott D. James
Industrial & Manufacturing Systems Engineering Department
GMI Engineering & Management Institute

Introduction to the Internet for Engineers and Computer Scientists

CHAPTER 1

Introducing the Internet

SCIENCE/ENGINEERING SPOTLIGHT: COMPUTER INTEGRATED MANUFACTURING

Computers have always been tools used to support the manufacturing process. Ordering and maintaining inventories, creating job lots and supporting the paper trail associated with these activities are examples of their common applications. Today, manufacturing is taking a proactive approach to employing computers in the manufacturing process. Computers no longer merely support the process; they are integrated into it.

Engineers have tried to create the one-model concept in which any manufactured product is conceptualized, designed, prototyped and put into production from one set of "data" stored on computer systems. This data is comprised of the actual part geometry, manufacturing specifications and machining instructions. While the one-model concept is not presently here in totality, many companies have successfully embraced computer integrated manufacturing and are very close to achieving that goal.

Objectives

The Internet is an incredible resource that you, as a student, need to learn to use! How would you like to be able to do all, or most, of the research for a paper or project from a single computer, grab the data and massage it right into the word processing package that you write with? Do you have an old computer and you just can't buy software for it anymore? Do you ever run into technical questions that no one you know seems to be able to answer, making you wish you had access to experts? If you have answered "yes" to any of these questions, then the Internet is the place you have been looking for.

Everyone talks about the Internet today. We are inundated as we watch television, seeing commercials with www.this and www.that. Are you online? What's your e-mail address? Did you look at that company's web site for information? These are the common types of questions you may be asked today. The purpose of this text is to help you learn about the different services that are available on the Internet. In addition, you will learn some of the jargon so that you may begin understanding and using some of the buzzwords that are flying around today.

This text makes only one assumption: that you have some type of access to the Internet. This book will not discuss how to get connected, nor will it discuss every different package that is available. These items are best left to your instructor, who can tell you what resources are made available to you by your school.

This chapter begins by examining the history of the Internet. A quick tour of the culture and etiquette of the Internet is also provided, along with a discussion of the general advantages and disadvantages of using the Internet. The chapter concludes with a discussion of some of the more technical issues surrounding the Internet.

1.1 HISTORY

Soon after commercial computers became available in the late 1950s, there was almost immediately a need to allow them to communicate with one another. In the late 1960s, the U.S. government realized the importance of allowing their research and development sites to electronically "talk" to one another. If the computers at various installations were connected, then files and data could be transferred much quicker than by courier or mail services.

The government-funded Advanced Research Projects Agency created ARPANET in 1969 to allow military and government installations performing research to communicate over phone lines. ARPANET originally had four computers networked together, and this was destined to become the original model of the Internet.

Another key piece of today's Internet came from ARPA: TCP/IP. TCP/IP stands for Transmission Control Protocol/Internet Protocol and is simply a set of standards that describe how data is to be transferred between computers. TCP/IP is the common tongue that computers that are to be on the Internet must speak. There are TCP/IP implementations for UNIX, MS-DOS, Windows (3.x, NT and 95), Macintosh and just about any other computer you can think of.

Eventually ARPANET went away from being purely government and military sites; educational and corporate entities also realized the benefits of being able to pool computer resources and share information. This collection of computers all over the world owned by individuals, companies, schools, governments, military organizations and the hardware necessary to link those same computers together form the Internet as we know it today.

A commonly asked question is, "Who runs the Internet?" No one person, group or organization owns it. The backbone of it is funded by the National Science Foundation in the U.S. In addition, there is an Internet Engineering Task Force (IETF) and Internet Advisory Board (IAB) who help to set standards for those who wish to connect to, and use, the Internet. The IAB makes its standards publicly available. These documents are known as RFC (Request for Comment) documents.

Another organization, MERIT, which is based near the University of Michigan in Ann Arbor, Michigan, was empowered by the National Science Foundation to upgrade and maintain the physical network (wiring, modems, switches and other related hardware items) of the Internet. It was MERIT who first suggested allowing the Internet to carry commercial traffic.

The Internet is growing at exponential rates: In the early 1980s there were 213 hosts on the Internet; in 1986 there were around 2,300; today there are literally millions. June, 1991 is another important date in the Internet's history, as it was the first time that the business use of the Internet exceeded its academic use.

1.2 INTERNET CULTURE

Initially the Internet was designed to allow folks access to computer resources that they might not have available to them at their own facilities and to allow the transfer of information between computers. Originally the primary users were researchers, scientists and engineers.

Today the Internet carries information (which could be in any format from text to digitized video) on every topic conceivable. Everyone from your neighbor to the President has access to the Internet, which consequently means that some of the wrong people can have access to the wrong information. There are computer crackers and criminals using the Internet for their own illicit gains at the same time that school children are watching satellite feeds from NASA.

You should cautiously choose the words that you use on the Internet—it is viewed as an electronic version of the real world. You will encounter people from many cultures with different perspectives. If you offend someone you may get in the middle of a flame war (a term we will discuss later on). Just be aware that there are as many different types of people on the Internet as there are in the physical world; most users are friendly, but there are others who can be abusive.

1.3 GENERAL NETIQUETTE

There are certain conventions and jargon that have been developed. If you pick up any of the many monthly magazines on the Internet, it seems as though the 'Net has a life of its own. The following is a list of suggestions that can hopefully make your transition to using the Internet a little less painful.

- Use the FAQs: Many mailing lists and newsgroups put together FAQs (Frequently Asked Questions). Always get the FAQ and read it first, if one is available. Once you start using services like mailing lists or UseNet News, you'll find references and instructions on how to get the FAQ.
- Avoid posting test messages. Don't waste people's time or Internet bandwidth with this kind of junk. You will find out if you can post when you try your first real message. If you absolutely must know if you can post, you should use one of the test newsgroups. See the section on UseNet News for details.
- Reply to questions. If you know the answer, share your knowledge. This is how the Internet has grown. If someone has personally e-mailed you and you don't know the answer, you should still send a reply just out of respect.
- Avoid flame wars! Flame wars occur on mailing lists and newsgroups when one person doesn't like what someone else said. The second person then sends a nasty little note back to the first person and the flame war begins. All that flame wars do is waste time and resources. If you really have a need to respond to a person that flames you, the least you can do is take it away from the group or list and use private e-mail.
- If you change electronic addresses make sure that you unsubscribe your old address to mailing lists and update the new address to lists and resources such as InterNIC.
- Abbreviations: Many messages on the Internet will contain strange looking abbreviations. Here are some that you may run across:

BRB (be right back)	BTW (by the way)
CU (see you)	FOAF (friend of a friend)
FYI (for your information)	IMHO (in my humble opinion)
IMO (in my opinion)	L8R (later)
MOTAS (member of the appropriate sex)	
MOTOS (member of the opposite sex)	
MOTSS (member of the same sex)	OB (as a prefix, obligatory)
OTOH (on the other hand)	PD (public domain)
SO (significant other)	ROTFL (rolling on the floor laughing)
RTFM (read the freaking manual)	WRT (with respect to)
<G> (grin)	

- Shouting: ANYTIME YOU TYPE IN ALL CAPS, IT IS ASSUMED YOU ARE SHOUTING. If you want to make a *point,* type a special character before and after the point that you want to make. Finally, @#$%^ looks a lot better in print than real profanity.
- Surfing and Lurking: Surfers are those Internet users who cover a lot of Internet territory and typically are helpful to other Internet users. Lurkers are those folks who use resources such as newsgroups but don't respond to questions. There is nothing wrong with being either of the two extremes.
- Smileys (or emoticons) show up in text messages and are used to convey feelings. Here are a few and their meanings:

<table>
<tr><td>:-)</td><td>smiling</td><td>:-D</td><td>laughing</td></tr>
<tr><td>;-)</td><td>winking</td><td>:-(</td><td>frowning</td></tr>
<tr><td>:-}</td><td>grinning</td><td>:-]</td><td>smirking</td></tr>
<tr><td>:-I</td><td>indifferent</td><td>:-#</td><td>smiley with braces</td></tr>
<tr><td>:-{)</td><td>smiley with mustache</td><td>{:-)</td><td>smiley with a toupee</td></tr>
<tr><td>:-X</td><td>my lips are sealed</td><td>=:-)</td><td>punk rocker smiley</td></tr>
<tr><td>=|:-)</td><td>Abraham Lincoln</td><td>:-o</td><td>surprise</td></tr>
<tr><td>:-@</td><td>screaming or yelling</td><td>8-)</td><td>eyeglasses</td></tr>
<tr><td>:-/</td><td>perplexed</td><td>;-7</td><td>tongue sticking out</td></tr>
</table>

1.4 ADVANTAGES AND DISADVANTAGES OF THE INTERNET

As with most resources publicly available, there are both advantages and disadvantages to working with the Internet. The following two lists summarize the key points:

GENERAL ADVANTAGES OF USING THE INTERNET:

- Information on the Internet can be accessed when it is most convenient for the user. There is no time that the Internet is closed. If you work best at 3:30 a.m. - go for it!
- The Internet is "blind" to race, religion, sex and creed.
- The direct cost to most academic users is only their time. The resources on the Internet have been paid for by those organizations who are registered on the Internet and by groups such as the National Science Foundation.
- Since the primary form of communication on the Internet is in writing, messages tend to be better organized and more productive than verbal communications.

GENERAL DISADVANTAGES OF THE INTERNET:

- Cautions must be placed on information received from the Internet—how credible is it? Some people tend to believe that anything that comes from a computer must be right. In addition, nasty little critters such as computer viruses could be picked up from the Internet. See Chapter 8 for details on dealing with these issues.

- While the direct cost to academic users may be next to nothing, other non-academic users might have to pay for communications to the Internet through fees such as long distance bills, Internet service provider organizations, and so forth.
- The Internet is fun, therefore it is addictive. Folks who would never think about wasting time at work or school can get involved in non-productive pursuits on the Internet that can add up to hours of time.
- Written communications may not be as clear as verbal communications. Some people are poorer writers than they are speakers. In addition, some people will write messages that they would never say face-to-face to another person.
- Mistakes can be amplified on the Internet. If you incorrectly state something on a mailing list, for example, several hundred (or thousand) people may see it.
- Finally, some people become information hoarders. Computer resources such as hard drive space, printer toner, printer paper and so forth can be quickly used up. In general, if something was easy to get once, you can probably get it pretty easily again. If something that is important to you was difficult to get, write down how and where you got it. That'll save trees, your hard drive space and your sanity from information hoarding and overload.

1.5 TECHNICAL ISSUES

If you are using your school's or company's computer resources, chances are that the following issues will be handled by some systems administrator in your Information Systems department. When reading an Internet or UNIX book, however, you will most likely run across these terms at some time. Let's spend a second examining each of the terms and their related issues.

Hosts: Hosts are computers on the Internet that provide some service (such as e-mail, file transfer, web site, etc.). A host may provide a single service or multiple services.

Hostname: All computers which are registered on the Internet have a unique hostname and a domain name. The domain name helps to identify the entity that the computer belongs to. For example, my primary system is *nova.gmi.edu.* The *gmi.edu* is the domain name—it identifies that my domain is an educational entity first (the *.edu*), and secondly GMI, which is the school's name. The *nova* part is the actual computer name. GMI actually has several computers that can connect to the Internet and each one has its own name: *nova.gmi.edu, defiant.gmi.edu, corvette.gmi.edu* among others. Some of the other extensions you will run across include:

.com - commercial or corporate entities

.mil - military

.gov - government

.net - Internet access providers

.org - non-profit organizations

The President is even on the air at *president@white-house.gov.* Since the U.S. started the Internet, we don't have a country extension added to the end of our hostnames. Foreign countries will, however; any hostname ending with **.fr** indicates the computer is in France, **.ca** indicates Canada and so on.

IP Address: Most computers on the Internet have a hostname; all computers on the Internet must have an IP address. The IP address is a unique number that identifies a specific computer. This is the way that communications traffic gets routed to the right computer. Without these numbers there would be no way to know which computer is which. IP addresses for computers that are on the Internet are handed out by the Internet Network Information Center (InterNIC) with which you must register to become a registered host on the Internet (your personal computer doesn't fall under this classification). The number will appear as four groups of three numbers such as 192.138.137.2 which is *nova*'s IP Address. Why have both hostnames and IP addresses? Hostnames are just convenient nicknames for our use so that we don't have to try to remember all the IP addresses. All hostnames get converted into their unique IP address for communication data routing purposes.

Ports & Sockets: Every computer that provides a service on the Internet listens on what are called ports. For example, any standard e-mail connection will be listened for on port 25. It wouldn't be very advantageous for a computer to only allow one e-mail connection at a time; in fact there may be times when multiple e-mailings are occurring simultaneously. How can this happen? The answer is through what is called a socket. Once the port detects that someone wishes to perform an e-mailing task, the computer creates a socket for each particular user wishing to e-mail. This is similar to the phone system in a company, in that, when you want to make a call you pick up the phone. The phone system is responsible for locating an open line for you to use. The phone system listens for a phone to be picked up (port) and provides you with a line (socket).

TCP/IP: TCP/IP stands for Transmission Control Protocol/Internet Protocol. This is a fancy name for what amounts to a standard way that all computers on the Internet communicate with one another. If you intend to be on the Internet, then your computer must speak TCP/IP. Essentially what TCP/IP does is break the data that is to be transmitted into little bundles called packets. TCP/IP sets the standards for what these packets should look like and how to get them from the source computer to the target computer and vice-versa. In addition, TCP/IP sets standards for certain types of computer connections and applications, such as Telnet and FTP, which we will examine in a couple of chapters from now.

UNIX: UNIX is a popular operating system for computers. It runs on everything from PCs to mainframes. Should you learn UNIX? It does tend to make using the Internet easier, since most of the original TCP/IP computers did run UNIX. Do you have to become a UNIX expert? No more than what you need to know about DOS if you are a Windows user. Most of the bigger sites on the Internet today still run UNIX since it comes with TCP/IP built in. UNIX was designed to be an open operating system, which embodies the idea of the Internet, so naturally the two go hand in hand. The more that you learn about UNIX and its quirks, the better equipped you are to handle the Internet and some of its quirks.

Client/Server: Look at three different books and chances are you will see three different definitions for this term. The easiest way to view client/servers is that a server provides some resource (such as an e-mail server). A client hooks up to the server and uses that resource (such as your PC using your company's e-mail system).

Chapter Summary

This chapter provided a brief overview of the founding of the Internet and what electronic life is like on the Internet. While there are some disadvantages to using the Internet, its positives more than compensate for any of the negatives. The chapter concluded with a section that defined some of the common terms and technical issues that are often encountered when reading Internet material.

Key Terms

Address
Computer
FAQ
Flame Wars
Hosts
Internet
Netiquette
Smileys
TCP/IP

CHAPTER

2

E-Mail & Finding Addresses

SCIENCE/ENGINEERING SPOTLIGHT: STEREO LITHOGRAPHY

How would you like to create an assembled product from some plastic goo? That's what rapid prototyping machines do. A specific type is the stereo lithography machine, in which plastic polymers are built up layer by layer and cut with a laser. When the process is finished, a working plastic prototype of a product has been created. The really interesting feature of all of this is that the prototype can have moving parts in it that do not have to be assembled. Some examples of items that have been created with stereo lithography machines include gear brains, bells with clappers attached and exhaust manifolds, just to name a few. It is projected that by the year 2000, stereo lithography machines will be about the size of a laser printer and will be able to create parts with sizes of up to one cubic foot in volume. This would allow designers to create their part geometry in a CAD/CAM package, send the design data to the stereo lithography machine and in a few hours, see a prototype of their design.

OBJECTIVES

This chapter looks at the process of sending electronic messages to other people, which is called e-mail. A discussion of how to locate other people's e-mail addresses through a number of different sources available on the Internet will be examined. This chapter also looks at how to send items other than text messages through e-mail. The chapter then concludes with some of the legal issues and etiquette that should be followed when e-mailing.

2.1 E-MAIL

E-mail (electronic mail) is one of the earliest uses of computer networking and communications. Put simply, e-mail allows you to send an electronic message to someone.

WHO CAN I E-MAIL?

- A single user
- A group of people
- A mailing list

WHAT CAN I E-MAIL?

- A message
- A file (pictures, programs, etc.)

WHAT ARE THE ADVANTAGES OF E-MAIL?

- It's fast and efficient
- It's cheaper than a stamp or a long-distance call
- You can create the message at your convenience
- It's global in scope (the Internet is world-wide)
- It doesn't add to the office paper problem

WHAT DO I NEED TO BE ABLE TO E-MAIL?

- You need the e-mail address of the person you are going to send the message to
- You should provide your return e-mail address
- The item(s) you want to e-mail
- Some form of e-mail program to perform the actual mailing. It may be a standalone program or part of another application, such as a web browser.

A Sample Text-Based E-Mail Session

Many e-mail packages such as PINE or ELM on UNIX systems, PEGASUS mail or EUDORA on PCs and Macs provide a menu system that shows you the various options that are available to you. The e-mailers will also prompt you for information as it is needed. You should check out what e-mail packages are available for you to use and choose one that you like. All e-mail packages basically require two pieces of information: the electronic address of the person that you want to send e-mail to and the message itself. Let's take a look at sending a sample e-mail message.

The first thing that I do is start up the e-mail package and tell it that I want to send a message. The bold typing indicates what I have typed in.

```
Mailbox is '/var/spool/mail/sjames' with 0 messages [ELM 2.4 PL24]




       |=pipe, !=shell, ?=help, <n>=set current to n, /=search pattern
 a)lias, C)opy, c)hange folder, d)elete, e)dit, f)orward, g)roup reply, m)ail,
 n)ext, o)ptions, p)rint, q)uit, r)eply, s)ave, t)ag, u)ndelete, or e(x)it

Command: Mail
To: vjames@nova.gmi.edu
```

The e-mail package then puts me into an editor where I can type my message. Once I am finished typing it, I will save my message and then send it.

```
    Hey V!  I was wondering if you had a chance to look at the network
    response problem yet.

    Thanks,
    Scott

    And now: s
         e)dit message, h)eaders, c)opy, i)spell, !)shell, s)end, or f)orget
    File /tmp/snd.19521 saved.
```

After sending the e-mail message, I can then follow the menu options to quit the e-mail program. Once the mail program has sent the mail to user *vjames,* she will receive some sort of notification that she has new mail. Let's assume that she reads the mail and sends a reply back to me. If I am on the system, I may receive a notice that says something like `You have new mail.` If I am not on the system, I will probably receive the same notice the next time that I log in.

Once I receive the notice that I have new mail, I can enter the mail program to read it:

```
Mailbox is '/var/spool/mail/sjames' with 1 message [ELM 2.4 PL24]


  N  1   Aug 13 V James         (20)   System Response
     2   Aug 12 lblasdell@lite (43)   Graphics Problems...
```

```
      |=pipe, !=shell, ?=help, <n>=set current to n, /=search pattern
a)lias, C)opy, c)hange folder, d)elete, e)dit, f)orward, g)roup reply, m)ail,
  n)ext, o)ptions, p)rint, q)uit, r)eply, s)ave, t)ag, u)ndelete, or e(x)it

Command:
```

I can now press the return key to view the contents of the message:

```
Message 1/1  From V James                       Aug 13, 96 11:15:38 am -0400

Return-Path: vjames
Subject: System Response
To: sjames@defiant.gmi.edu (Scott James)
Date: Tue, 13 Aug 1996 11:15:38 -0400 (EDT)

Scott,

I haven't looked at the problem yet.  Hope to get to it today sometime.

V



Command ('i' to return to index):
```

At this point, I can return to the menu and quit the e-mail program. Most e-mail packages that are available today have a very similar menu-based interface to make their use as easy as possible.

A Sample Graphical-Based E-Mailer Session

As stated above, there are many graphical-based e-mailers available. This section will take a peek at Eudora, which is a popular graphical e-mailer available for Microsoft Windows and the Macintosh. As with most graphical e-mailers, Eudora is very easy to use and has some very nice features built in. Eudora will display a mailbox and play a little tune whenever the user receives new mail. The following is a sample screen of what Eudora looks like:

Whenever a user wants to use Eudora, that user must log on to the system with a username and password. This allows Eudora to confirm that only authorized users are reading their respective e-mail. After the user has successfully logged on, Eudora will then allow the user to read or send e-mail. Notice how much more intuitive working with Eudora is versus the text-based e-mailer.

Once I've logged in, if I want to read my mail, I simply select the Mailbox menu option followed by the Inbox choice. The following screen shows a list of the messages that I have in my "inbox."

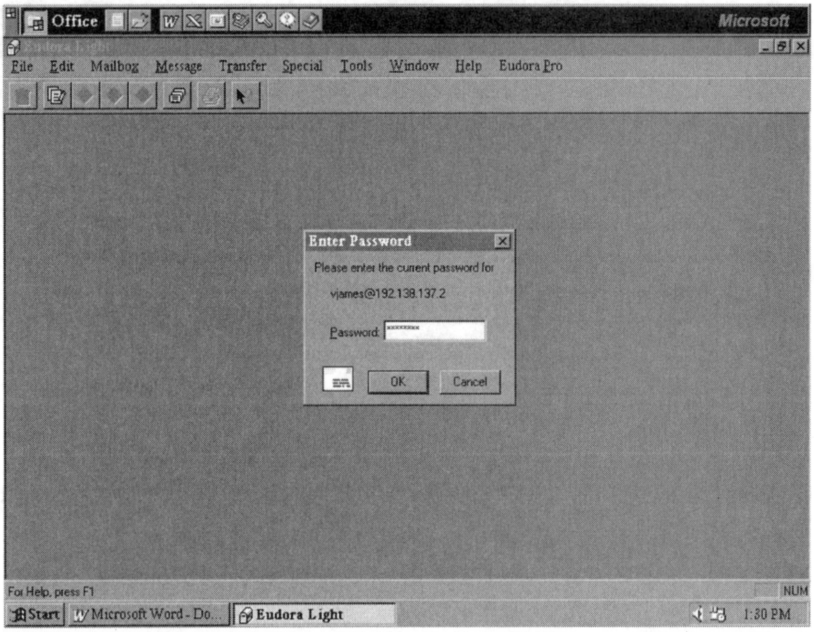

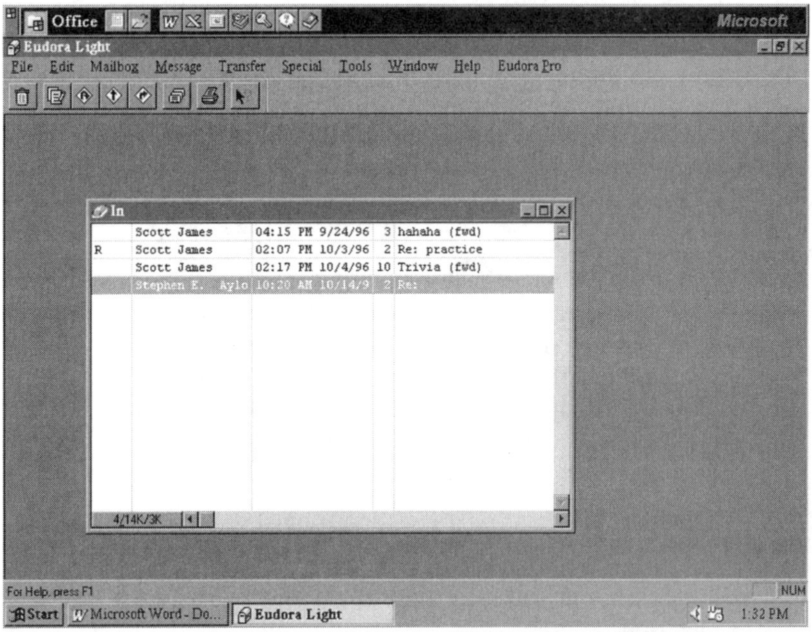

If I want to read a message, I simply point at the message with my mouse and double click on the message itself. Here is the e-mail message that I received:

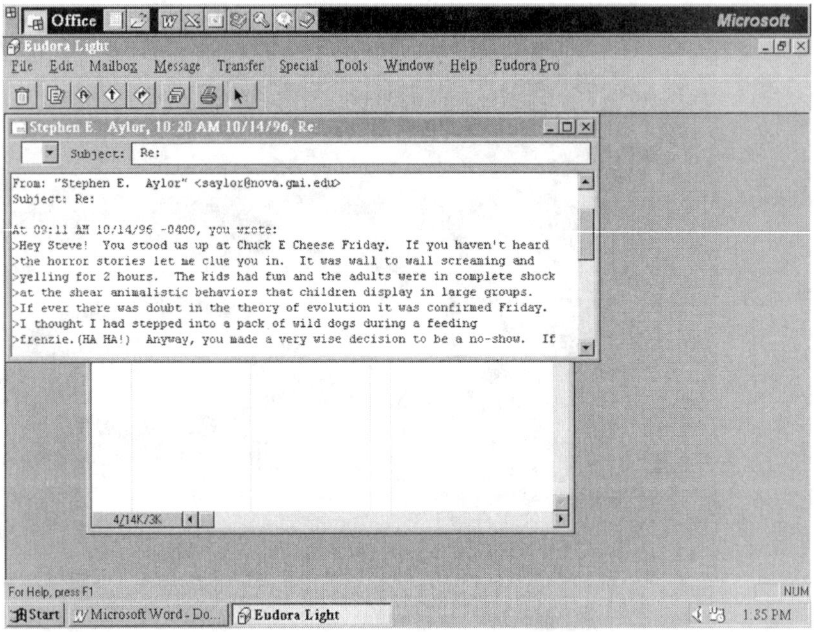

As you can see, Eudora is a lot nicer to work with than most text-based e-mailers. Sending an e-mail message from Eudora is very easy too: I simply select the Message menu option followed by New. The following screen then pops up. You should be familiar with the information that Eudora needs such as the To:, From: and Subject: lines from our discussion above. Once I have typed my message in, I simply press the Send button to send the message off.

PRACTICE!

Let's try out our e-mailing skills by sending a message to a mail server that will e-mail a quotation from an almanac back to us. We want to send the e-mail to the address *almanac@oes.orst.edu.* If your e-mailer wants a subject line, leave it blank. Some e-mailers will ask you if you want to continue with a blank subject line; if yours does, just answer yes. The body of the message should say *send quote.*

In a little while, you will receive a mail message back from the almanac server which you can read in your e-mail package.

2.2 HOW DO I FIND A PERSON'S E-MAIL ADDRESS?

A common task that you may need to do when e-mailing is trying to locate another user's electronic address. There are 6 different ways that you can try to find this information.

1) Finger: Finger is a fairly standard TCP/IP program that will provide you with basic information about a user on a system. The typical syntax is *finger username@do-*

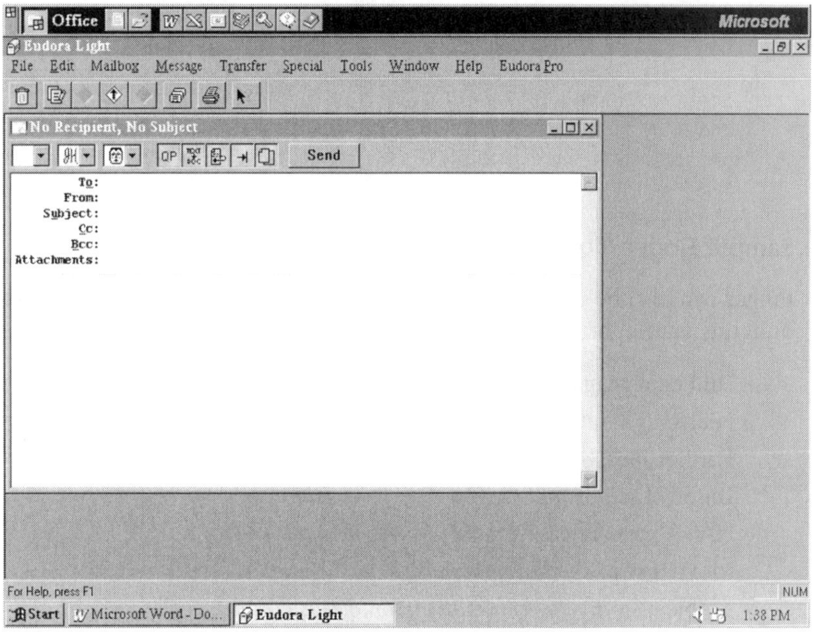

main.name. To use this though, you have to either know the person's username or at least the domain name of the computer that the person uses. An example is *finger sjames@nova.gmi.edu.* This will bring back information about me. Let's say that you don't know my username, but you do know what the domain name is; you could type *finger @nova.gmi.edu.* Unfortunately, this will return finger information on everyone currently logged onto *nova.gmi.edu* besides myself, if I am even on the system.

A Sample Finger Command

```
nova{sjames}1% finger @nova.gmi.edu
[nova.gmi.edu]
Login       Name               TTY Idle    When     Where
khicks   Kim A. Hicks          p7    33 Fri 08:29  192.138.137.190
Jtandy   John Tandy            p8 3:39 Fri 07:39  tandy
hgholmes Harry Gholmes         pb       Fri 11:44  CURLY
sjames   Scott D. James        pf       Fri 11:46  beopst
```

You can see that the last line shows my username, "real name," when I logged in, and from where I am logged in. If you specify a username after the finger command, you can get detailed information on a particular user.

```
nova{sjames}3% finger sjames@nova.gmi.edu
Login name: sjames                      In real life: Scott D. James
Directory: /faculty/sjames              Shell: /usr/local/bin/tcsh
On since Apr 30 11:46:48 on ttypf from beopst
Mail last read Fri Apr 30 11:46:51
```

```
Project: If you have to ask, I won't tell you...
Plan:
-----------------------------------------------------------------
Scott D. James
Industrial & Manufacturing Systems Engineering Department
GMI Engineering & Management Institute     Internet: sjames@nova.gmi.edu
-----------------------------------------------------------------
```

Sample Finger Sites to Try

Finger can also be used to return more than just usernames. Some sites offer lists and bulletins via finger. Here are a few examples:

Billboard Magazine charts: *buckmr@rpi.edu*
Nielson TV ratings: *normg@halcyon.halcyon.com*
Earthquakes: *quake@geophys.washington.edu*
Baseball scores: *jtchern@ocf.berkeley.edu*
NASA press releases: *nasanews@space.mit.edu*
Movie trivia: *cyndiw@magnus1.com*
Tropical storms: *forecast@typhoon.atmos.colostate.edu*
Northern lights: *aurora@xi.uleth.ca*
Coke™ machine: *@coke.elab.cs.cmu.edu*
  M&M™: *mnm@coke.elab.cs.cmu.edu*
  Graph: *bargraph@coke.elab.cs.cmu.edu*
Buy a Coke™: *coke@cs.wisc.edu*
Almanac: *copi@oddjob.uchicago.edu*
Weather: *weather@cirrus.mit.edu*

PRACTICE!

Try out one or two of the addresses given above, such as `finger coke@cs.wisc.edu`.

2) Use InterNIC's White Pages Database: Though incomplete, this may become the global address directory of the future. InterNIC tries to weld several of the lookup utilities together under a common menu. To use the InterNIC white pages, Telnet to *ds.internic.net* and log-in as *guest* and you will then receive information about how to search for a user. (See Chapter 4 for information on how to use Telnet.) InterNIC's service is menu-driven, so read the screens and follow the prompts.

If you want information about InterNIC, you can send e-mail to *info@internic.net*. If you want to add yourself to the InterNIC database, send a message to *admin@ds.internic.net* and ask to be added to the White Pages.

The following screen gives you an idea of what to expect when you connect to InterNIC (and after you survive the onslaught of configuration questions, most of which can be answered by pressing the enter key):

```
InterNIC Directory and Database Services (DS) Telnet Application
                           Main Menu

        1) User Tutorial
        2) InterNIC Directory of Directories
        3) InterNIC Directory Services ("White Pages")
        4) Search the InterNIC DS Server File Space
        5) Browse the InterNIC DS Server File Space (GOPHER)
        6) Internet Public File Search (ARCHIE)
        7) Internet Documentation (RFC's, FYI's, etc.) Search
        8) End Application (or 'q', 'e', 'quit', or 'exit')

Enter option (1-8) or 'q' (to end session) and press <RETURN>:
```

3) WHOIS: WHOIS is the original InterNIC white pages program. This program is one of the provided options available through InterNIC as mentioned above. To use WHOIS, you should enter as much of the person's name as you can. If anything in the WHOIS database matches what you typed in, that information will be returned to you. The easiest way to use WHOIS is to Telnet to a WHOIS server (a list of WHOIS servers can be obtained by anonymous FTP to *sipb.mit.edu.* The file */pub/whois/whois-servers.list* contains the information. See Chapter 4 for information on how to use FTP.) You can also Telnet to *whois.internic.net* and log-in as *whois*. Another WHOIS server that you can Telnet to is *nic.ddn.mil* (start WHOIS by typing *whois*; there is no login or password required).

The second way to access WHOIS is to send an e-mail message to one of the WHOIS servers, such as *mailserv@ds.internic.net* with no subject. The body of the message should be a single command of the following format *whois [-h hostname] username.* The *-h hostname* portion is optional. By supplying a hostname, you can help WHOIS cut down on duplicate data such as looking for a user with the name John Smith. Obviously there may be several John Smiths, so the hostname will help to confine the search. If you supply just the username in the message, you may want to put a period in front of the username, such as *whois .sjames.* The period lets the WHOIS server know that you are talking about a person and not a host.

The third way to access WHOIS is to try typing the *whois* command directly. Many UNIX systems have a copy of this program and it is a very convenient way to access a WHOIS server without having to resort to Telnet or e-mail.

The final way to access WHOIS is to locate a gopher site that supports WHOIS searches. (Chapter 5 deals with gophers.)

If you would like to become registered in the WHOIS database, either FTP the file */netfile/user-template.txt* from *nic.ddn.mil* or get the file via e-mail by sending a message to *service@nic.ddn.mil*; put the filename *user-template.txt* in the subject line. After you have obtained the file, fill it out and e-mail it to *registrar@nic.ddn.mil.*

4) Netfind: Netfind doesn't rely on databases of gathered information like InterNIC's WHOIS solution. Netfind actually goes out onto the Net and looks at network gateways and asks if the gateway has heard of the user that is being searched for.

Netfind requires two pieces of information: the user's real name or login name and a location for the user (a hostname, city, state, etc.). Netfind may or may not return any information since some sites do not permit this kind of information to be queried.

To use Netfind, Telnet to *ds.internic.net* and log-in as *guest.* The system will provide instructions and provide you instruction on Netfind's use.

Alternately, many UNIX computers now have a Netfind program running directly on them. If you are on a UNIX computer, you might want to investigate this option since it provides a convenient front end to a Netfind server without having to resort to Telneting.

Here is a list of some other U.S. Netfind sites that can be Telneted to (login as *netfind*):

bruno.cs.colorado.edu

ds.internic.net

eis.calstate.edu

hto-e.usc.edu

mudhoney.micro.umn.edu

netfind.oc.com

redmont.cis.uab.edu

5) Knowbot Information Service (KIS): KIS doesn't maintain its own database; instead it queries the other databases that are already available (Finger, MCI Mail's directory, Finger, WHOIS and so forth). By providing a single point for you to supply information on the individual you are trying to locate, you can search multiple sources while having to supply the information only once. All information returned will be massaged into a single format so that all information sources are uniform in their presentation.

You can either Telnet to a KIS server or e-mail a server to access the KIS service; for example Telnet to *nri.reston.va.us 185.* The 185 is required since this specifies that port 185 on that computer is for the KIS service. Other KIS servers are available; a list is on the *nri.reston.va.us* computer (two other U.S. KIS servers are *info.cnri.reston.va.us 185* and *regulus.cs.bucknell.edu 185*).

To e-mail the KIS server, send a message to *netadress@nri.reston.va.us* (or *mitwp@mit.edu*). The body should contain one or more of the following keywords with the appropriate data attached:

- Identifier which says to use the information supplied after the keyword Identifier for the search rather than the username. This is often used when specifying a user ID number instead of a name, which is how companies like CompuServe and MCI Mail work.
- Org specifies the organization to which the person belongs and should be either a full or partial domain name.
- Query provides the username to search for.

An example would be:

```
org gmi.edu
query sjames
```

6) UseNet User List: Anyone that contributes to UseNet News has their name and address collected by a server at MIT (which is where UseNet started). Since many folks read and contribute to UseNet, this data may be particularly useful when trying to locate a user's address.

To query the list by e-mail, send a message to *mail-server@pit-manager.mit.edu.* There is no subject; the body of the message should be *send usenet-address/username.* For example *send usenet-address/james* would return all UseNet users recorded with the last name of James.

If you're not sure of the exact spelling of a person's name, you should include several send lines in the message. That will help cut down on the amount of time you spend searching.

2.3 FILES AND E-MAIL

In the world of computers there are two kinds of files: theirs (the computer's, that is) and ours. Ours are nice and readable, like our e-mail messages. Theirs are weird looking combinations of characters that, as far as we're concerned, can't possibly make any sense. Examples of "their" files that are useful to us include graphic pictures, sound files and programs. But for us to try and read them, the files look like junk. This is the concept of text (or ASCII) versus binary files.

It is obviously advantageous to be able to e-mail binary files. Think about a huge spreadsheet that you wrote in Excel on a PC in New York. Your L.A. office needs it **now** for their Macintosh. If you sent a disk overnight it would take too long and someone would have to be able to read the PC disk and pull the file off of it for the Mac. You decide to put e-mail to the rescue. The only problem is that most e-mailers will only send text messages. Text messages are what are known as 7-bit ASCII (or characters 0 - 127); binary files are 8-bit (or characters 0 - 255).

Your solution to this dilemma is to employ a program know as uuencode. Uuencode will take each 0 - 255 character in your binary file and convert it into two 0 - 127 characters. When this process is done, you can then send what appears to the e-mailer as a plain text file. When the person on the other end receives the file, they will run a program called uudecode to convert the file from text mode back into binary mode.

Let's look at how I would uuencode my spreadsheet called 1995sale.xls:

```
uuencode 1995sale.xls < 1995sale.xls > 1995sale.uue
```

What this command does is uuencodes a file which will be called 1995sale.xls (the first one shown) from a file called 1995sale.xls (the second one shown) into 1995sale.uue (the uuencoded file). Why do I have the two 1995sale.xls? It permits computer systems that have filename limitations to work together. For example uuencode pcname.zip < alongunixname.zip > pcname.uue. Since MS-DOS files are limited to 8 characters and an optional 3 character extension and UNIX files can have multiple extensions and filenames longer than 8 characters, we normally would have a problem with the differing requirements imposed on filenames. Fortunately uuencode provides us with a workaround.

The person on the other end could then decode the file they received by typing:

```
uudecode 1995sale.uue
```

After that command has run, the file 1995sale.xls will appear back in its original format.

How do I know if a file has been uuencoded? Typically the file will look like someone stepped on their keyboard while typing your e-mail message. You may see something like the following:

```
This is the 1995 sales projection spreadsheet in uuencoded form.
-----------------------------------------------------------------------

begin 644 1995sale.xls
M'XL1%329J-123(*#!KA(SK(@KS(D!KE!@EKWE(!Q]{ASDASD:)
ASDASKD!((QKQ*&KJ!@:L:!@"> @!{!(S(A*SI@*(SIAS(@(@I#
```

The line that gives it away is the *begin* line. The 644 is just a UNIX permission number that's really not all that important to us. You can see that the original filename appears on the *begin* line as well. This is how uudecode knows what to call the decoded file.

A final note—file compression: If you have a large file, you should perform some kind of compression on it. If you have a lot of files, you should put them into a single file archive and then compress it. The reason for this is that for every one character that is in the original file, two will appear in the encoded file. We will talk about common compression files in the section on FTP in Chapter 4.

2.4 E-MAIL LEGAL ISSUES AND ETIQUETTE

Be warned: anything you send electronically could either end up in the wrong place or more than the person intended to receive the mail may view it. Various courts have ruled differently on dealing with computer privacy issues. Some companies view e-mail and the use of their systems as company property. Even personal e-mail is seen as belonging to the company. Other companies don't see things this way: they feel that e-mail messages should be just as private and personal as real world mail. In either case there are some definite no-no's: copyright, mailing illegal material and libel.

- Anything that is copyrighted should not be electronically transferred since you are still making a copy of the original material, and that is illegal.
- Some types of material, even though they are not copyrighted, are illegal to send and receive, such as some forms of pornography.

- Libel, or slandering or defamation of a person's character, is as valid in electronic form as it is in any other.

The bottom line on e-mail concerns is this: if you wouldn't want anyone to see some piece of mail you have, just get rid of it! Be warned though, that deleting the mail from your account doesn't guarantee that it is completely gone. System backups of all files are regularly made on large systems. Also, there are some operating systems that don't physically delete files, they just mark the space as available, meaning that the deleted files could be retrieved.

Encryption

If you have a need for secure transmission of data, you may want to encrypt it before you send it. Typically you would encrypt the file first with an encryption program and then send it. There are a lot of programs available that do encryption:

- **ROT13** rotates all letters 13 locations, such that A becomes M. This is not a very advanced encryption scheme. You can duplicate the ROT13 program on any UNIX system which does not have it with the following command:

```
tr '[a-m] [n-z] [A-M] [N-Z]' '[n-z][a-m][N-Z][A-M]' < infile  > outfile
```

- **Word substitution** requires the encoder to enter a keyword that locks the file. The decoder must enter the same keyword before the file can be translated back to its original form.
- **DES standard encryption packages** use an algorithm to generate a key that is extremely difficult to break. This algorithm cannot be exported to most countries outside North America.
- **Public Key (PGP - Pretty Good Protection) Encryption** is a package in which you encode your message with one master key and individuals whom you trust are each given a unique key that will unlock the message. This is superior to word substitution since the people who will do the decoding don't know your keyword. This enables you to verify that the message did come from you. This technique is also known as one-way encryption.

Etiquette

Just like any other form of communication, written or verbal, there are certain accepted principles that we use. E-mail is no exception! The following is a list of good e-mail practices to follow:

- Read your mail frequently.
- When replying, clearly identify yourself and the subject of the message.
- Make sure you write carefully spelling words correctly and using proper English.
- Know and respect your recipient; make sure you only write things that you would say face-to-face with the person.
- Keep the message to the point.

- Send to only those who need to receive it (avoid long lists).
- If you are replying to a message, reiterate what you are replying to. Also include only a few replies in the message New sent - otherwise, you start to create chain e-mail.
- Only mark Urgent items Urgent. Some e-mailers allow you to specify a priority. If you mark everything Urgent, nobody is going to pay special attention to anything you send.
- Never assume e-mail is private as previously mentioned. If you send it, it will go somewhere—wrong addresses usually end up at *postmaster@domain.name* or *root@domain.name.*

2.5 E-MAILING OUTSIDE THE INTERNET

With all the ways to get to the Internet, there must be ways to get outside of it. What happens if you want to correspond with an Internet-illiterate CompuServe user? That's the issue this section addresses. Let's look at the common computer services first, and then a list containing some of the not-so-common.

AMERICA ON-LINE

- To send to America On-line from the Internet follow this format: *userID@aol.com*
- To send from America On-line to the Internet use *username@domain.name*

COMPUSERVE

- To send to CompuServe addresses from the Internet, use the following format: *user.id@compuserve.com.* Make sure that you put a period in the user id instead of the usual comma. Commas mean special things to e-mailers, so we have to substitute with the period instead.
- To send from CompuServe to the Internet, a user must include the word Internet as part of the Send To line, such as: *internet: sjames@nova.gmi.edu*

GENIE

- To send to Genie from the Internet, use the following format: *username@genie.geis.com*
- To send from Genie to the Internet use: *username@domain.name@INET#*

MCI MAIL

- MCI Mail allows you to access users by their full name, username or user number. Unfortunately the user number is the only unique identifier. To send mail to MCI Mail from the Internet use the following format: *identifier@mcimail.com*

  The identifier could be:

```
sjames@mcimail.com
scott_james@mcimail.com
139230@mcimail.com
```

- For MCI Mail customers to send out to the Internet, they must include the following in their e-mail:

```
To:  person's real name
EMS:  internet
MBX: username@domain.name
```

Prodigy

- To send to a Prodigy user from the Internet, use the following format: *username@domain.name*
- To send from Prodigy to an Internet user, use: *username@domain.name*

Summary of Services and Required Formats

The following table provides a listing of how to communicate with some of the more popular online services from the Internet. This list is not complete, nor exhaustive. If you are interested in a much more comprehensive list, get a copy of John Chew's Internetwork Mail Guide which is FTP-able from *ftp.msstate.edu* in the */pub/docs* directory.

TABLE 2.1

Service	Send to a Service User	Send from the Service
America On-line	username@aol.com	username@domain.name
BITNET	username%site.bitnet@gateway Note: The gateway must be both an Internet and BITNET gateway	username@domain.name@gateway
CompuServe	nnnnn.nnn@compuserve.com	internet:username@domain.name
Delphi	username@delphi.com	in%"username@domain.name"
Genie	username@genie.geis.com	username@domain.name@INET#
MCI Mail	username@mcimail.com Note: users may have more than one non-unique name	Specify the recipient's name in the "To" section, "internet" in the "EMS" section and the full internet address in the "MBX" section
Prodigy	username@prodigy.com	username@domain.name
SprintMail		(C:USA,ADMD:TELEMAIL,PRMD: INTERNET,ID:<username(a) domain.name>)
UUNET	username%machine.domain.name@UUNET.UU.NET	username@domain.name

2.6 A FINAL NOTE ON E-MAIL

As you probably realize, sending text messages with e-mail is not a problem. We have to do some work up front to send binary files though. There is a new standard that is being worked on to solve this problem: MIME (Multipurpose Internet Mail Extension). In the near future, MIME will probably replace the Simple Mail Transport Protocol (SMTP), which is the current way that e-mail is exchanged.

MIME is not limited to messages containing only the characters 0 - 127. In fact, MIME specifically targets the following objects as being items that should be sendable through e-mail: text messages, programs, audio files, encapsulated messages, multipart messages, video and image data.

Soon e-mail users should be able to send just about any item through the mail. The recipient of the message will then be able to "see" that item just as easily as text messages are seen today. The big advantage is that no form of translation (such as uudecoding) will be necessary.

Chapter Summary

This chapter provided an overview of the most basic, but possibly the most important of Internet services, e-mail. A discussion of locating the electronic addresses of other people on the Internet was also provided. The chapter concluded with an examination of legal issues, e-mail etiquette and how files can be sent in e-mail. In addition, the chapter showed how an Internet user can send e-mail messages to other computer services beyond the Internet.

Key Terms

Address
Binary Files
e-mail
Encryption
finger
InterNic
Knowbot Information Service
MIME
Netfind
Text (ASCII) Files
UseNet User List
uudecode
uuencode
White Pages Database
WHOIS

Problems

1. Send an e-mail message to your instructor to show that you know how to use your e-mail system.
2. Send an e-mail message to a friend at another school. Ask him or her to send you a message in return and print that reply out.
3. Use the finger command and see if you can find out any information about your instructor. Print any returned information out.

4. Print out a copy of this week's NASA Press Releases, retrieved by fingering *nasanews@space.mit.edu.*
5. See if your instructor is in the WHOIS database. If he or she is, print out whatever information is displayed.
6. Try uuencoding a binary file of your instructor's choice. Mail the file to yourself and examine the message you receive. Save the message and then try uudecoding it.

CHAPTER

3

Mailing Lists & UseNet News

SCIENCE/ENGINEERING SPOTLIGHT: OPTICAL COMPUTERS

Computers are getting faster with each new generation of microprocessors. Just how fast can they get? How about the speed of light . . . Believe it or not, computers that are currently available are constrained by how fast electrical pulses can run down the wires. If the wires could be replaced by something else, the computer could work more quickly. Optical computing is the answer. Light and fiber optics will replace wires. Even the switches which are the integral part of the computer may someday be replaced by light switches. So if you think that the increase in speed from the original IBM-PC's 8088 Intel processor to today's Pentium has been immense, watch for the speed increases as optical computing becomes a reality.

OBJECTIVES

This chapter takes a look at working with mass text communications to other Internet users. The Internet provides two ways for this mass text media to occur: mailing lists and

UseNet News. Mailing lists are collections of text items on one particular subject that are mailed out to all of the members on a mailing list. You can think of this as an Internet magazine. UseNet News, on the other hand, is the Internet's daily press. The UseNet News has thousands of newsgroups and you can pick and choose which ones you want to read. Let's get started by looking at mailing lists.

3.1 MAILING LISTS

Mailing lists are another Internet service that you can utilize once you have e-mail access. The idea behind a mailing list is that it is similar to the computer bulletin board systems that were popular in the 1980s. A mailing list is a location where people that have a similar interest can get together and discuss that interest. There are mailing lists on just about any topic that you can imagine. The principle behind the operation of the mailing list is that you will use your e-mail address to subscribe to mailing lists and periodically you will receive an electronic message back from that mailing list.

Some mailing lists act like magazines, in that they gather a number of messages and then send out one long message. Others will send out every message received to each subscriber of that list every time that a new message is received. The general idea, in either case, is that people who are interested in a particular topic will subscribe to a mailing list. These same subscribers typically will e-mail messages, articles, et cetera to the mailing list moderator, who will in return have the mailing list server send out the mailing list message to all of the subscribers.

A mailing list performs three primary functions:

- The list administrator can use it to deliver information to the list subscribers.
- Subscribers to the list can send out information to all the other subscribers.
- You can post files to the list (remember to uuencode binary files) or retrieve files that other subscribers have posted.

How Do You Find What Mailing Lists Are Available?

A list of available mailing lists is available by anonymous FTP from *rtfm.mit.edu* in the */pub/usenet-by-group/news.lists* directory. The list is in 14 separate parts, each with a name like *Publicly_Accessible_Mailing_Lists,_Part_??_14*. You can also get a list back by e-mailing *listserv@vm1.nodak.edu* with the message *list global*. SRI has a mailing list that is anonymous FTP-able from *ftp.nisc.sri.com* in */netinfo/interest-groups.Z*.

How Do I Subscribe to a Mailing List?

Once you have some lists that you want to subscribe to, you need to locate the list server that handles that particular list and send some e-mail to subscribe to it. This information should have been included with whatever source told you about the mailing list. Typically the e-mail message will contain a blank subject line and the body of the message will contain the line *SUBSCRIBE listname yourrealname.*

For example, if I wanted to join the Thought For The Day mailing list on Texas A&M's LISTSERV, I would e-mail the following:

```
To: listserv@tamvml.tamu.edu
Subject:
Message:  SUBSCRIBE TFTD-L Scott James
```

If you were successful in subscribing to the list, you should receive a confirmation e-mail message back. The basics of subscribing to list servers are just that easy: all messages to the list server must be e-mailed, the subject line should always be blank and commands may be entered in either case.

One other note of importance: when you receive messages from the list server, you will notice that the address is slightly different than what you used when you subscribed to the list. For the example that I used above, I would receive a message back from *tftd-l@tamvml.tamu.edu.* What's the second address for? That is the list address! If I send a message to the list address, everyone who has subscribed to the mailing list will receive a copy of the message that I send to it. The original address is the list server address which I use when I want to send commands (such as subscribe) to the list server.

Other Mailing List Commands

There are several other commands that we will work with when using list servers. All LISTSERV type list servers can provide you with help and let you know about the lists that they carry. In addition, most can tell you about lists that are carried by other LISTSERVs.

To get help from a LISTSERV, send a message to the server address with the body saying *help* to bring back LISTSERV help information. To find out what lists are carried by a LISTSERV, send an e-mail message with the message body saying *list.* To do this at the Texas A&M LISTSERV, I would send the following e-mail message:

```
To:  listserv@tamvml.tamu.edu
Subject:
Message:  LIST
```

The returned message would contain only the lists maintained by the Texas A&M LISTSERV. To find out about all of the lists that this LISTSERV knows about, I would send the message *list global.* I will receive mail back with probably about 5,000 mailing lists that are available. If I wanted to confine the search a little bit, I could send a message that says *list global* and a particular topic. For example *list global business* would return any mailing lists dealing with business.

Some of the other commands that I could send to a LISTSERV type list server include:

signoff listname	(To unsubscribe to the list)
register yourrealname	(Registers your real name on the server so you don't have

	to keep including it with every subscribe command)
register off	(Won't report your name to anyone who performs a review)
review	(Lets you know who's subscribed to a particular list)
index	(Shows you a list of files on the server. You can retrieve them with *get listserv filename*)
info	(Shows you a list of files that are available on the server that are about the server. You can retrieve them with an e-mail message of *info filename* or *get listserv filename*.)

Note: You can include more than one command in an e-mail message!

How Do I Post a Message to a List I'm Subscribed to?

Simply sending any message to the mailing list address (not the list server address!) will get your message to the right location. The message will then either automatically be forwarded to all other subscribers or it will go to a list administrator who gathers the messages, condenses them down, and then periodically mails the information out in a list which has more of a magazine format.

3.2 USING MAJORDOMO MAILING LISTS

Majordomo lists are just a different type of list server. These types of lists aren't as widespread as LISTSERV lists. The concepts between using the two types of list servers are just about identical though.

Here is a list of the Majordomo commands:

subscribe listname yourrealname	(to subscribe to a list)
unsubscribe listname yourrealname	(to unsubscribe to a list)
help	(to get help on a list)
index	(to perform an index of the list server's files)

How Do I Find Majordomo Lists?

Sending an e-mail message to a Majordomo server with the message body *lists* will do the trick. One Majordomo site to get you started is *majordomo@vector.casti.com*. Another source of information on Majordomo list servers would be in the files which are maintained at MIT that were mentioned earlier.

Different Types of Lists

When you are working with lists, you may find that the lists are talked about in different categories. Here are the common categories and their meanings:

Moderated. These lists have a moderator who reads and approves all messages before they are posted to the list. These lists, consequently, stay more on track and are sometimes more informative than unmoderated lists.

Unmoderated. Whatever someone sends to the list address will appear on the list. The main problem here is that you may get bits and pieces of communications.

Digested. These type of lists collect large numbers of messages and then periodically mail out a more formatted presentation of the mailing list to the list's subscribers.

Undigested. You get each message from the list server as it is received. You could get bombarded with e-mail this way.

3.3 USENET NEWS

The UseNet News is kind of like having mailing lists on-line. UseNet News was originally an experiment at the University of North Carolina in 1979. Today there are literally millions of people who use UseNet daily, and for many, this is their view of the Internet. UseNet is really nothing more than a mechanism that allows groups to be formed and for discussions to be carried out within these groups. The nice thing about UseNet is that you can pick what groups you want to view and you will only see news messages as they are posted.

There are now more than 10,000 newsgroups on topics ranging from motorcycle repair to the newest Microsoft products that are out. If you are interested in a particular topic, chances are you will find a newsgroup to your liking. Since computer resources are limited, postings on these groups are usually kept only for two weeks or so. Thus, if you see something you are interested in, you had better read or download the article while you can.

UseNet is an extremely valuable resource to have access to. Since each group has a topic, you can ask technical questions of the group and receive responses from other individuals who are active and knowledgeable in that particular area.

UseNet doesn't physically exist anywhere. It's much more like the LISTSERV concept; i.e. there are news servers. Essentially, you will use some news reader software which will let you read messages, post messages and access the different groups. It's very much like e-mail in that regard. UseNet doesn't automatically send things to your mailbox; it's your responsibility to read the news and download what you want to keep. UseNet does support the uuencoding and uudecoding of binary files so that those types of files can be posted to a particular newsgroup.

Newsgroups typically have threads running in them. A thread is when someone asks a question and receives replies to that question. When other folks start replying to the first reply, a thread is born.

Sometimes threads and flame wars on newsgroups get out of hand. This is when it is important to know the capabilities of your news reader. Many news readers allow "killfiles" to be created. Killfiles are used to screen out threads or words or phrases that you don't want to see.

A Few Newsgroups

Here's a very small sampling of some of the newsgroups that are available:

misc.forsale	comp.unix.questions	comp.lang.c
rec.arts.movies	alt.folklore.urban	misc.education
misc.invest	alt.business.import-export	

What's in a Group Name?

Most groups have some prefix attached to them, as you can see above. Here's a list of the most common prefixes and what they mean:

- alt - usually more of an "underground" newsgroup such as alt.tasteless; however there are excellent alt groups such as alt.3d which has regular discussions on radiosity and ray tracing
- bionet - biology
- bit - topics from Bitnet
- biz - business, marketing and advertisements
- clari - Clarinet is real news provided by a private company which must be paid for, usually by the news server that wishes to carry these groups. In fact, in most cases, if you see any clari groups, someone has most likely paid for these groups to be carried for you, so feel free to use them.
- comp - computers
- gnu - Free Software Foundation and its GNU project
- ieee - Institute of Electrical and Electronic Engineering
- k12 - kindergarten through high school
- misc - newsgroups that don't fall into one of the other categories
- news - general news and topical items about UseNet itself
- rec - recreation, hobbies and the arts
- sci - science
- soc - social issues
- talk - debate oriented

Some newsgroups are jokes and may only appear for a day or two. An odd group name like *alt.swedish.chef.bork.bork.bork* probably is a joke.

There are also moderated newsgroups just like moderated mailing lists. The group moderator sorts out the messages before they are posted on the group. This tends to keep things on track, keep things tasteful and keep out the flame wars.

How Do I Get Started on UseNet?

Once you have a news reader and point it toward a news server, chances are it will have access to literally thousands of newsgroups, many of which you won't be interested in. Don't worry, you can unsubscribe to the ones that you don't want. There are several groups that you might want to examine for help in getting started with the UseNet News: *news.announce.newusers*, *news.answers*, *news.groups*, *news.newusers.questions*, and *news.software*.

news.announce.newusers regularly posts five articles that are of interest to new users:

- Answers to frequently asked questions about UseNet
- A primer on how to work with the UseNet community

- Rules for posting to UseNet
- Hints for writing style for UseNet
- Emily Postnews answers your questions on netiquette

News.answers serves two purposes for us: we can post questions about UseNet and almost all of the other newsgroups' FAQs can be found here.

What Are the Common Tasks I Can Perform on UseNet

The answer to this question is going to depend more on the news reader that you use than anything else. You should be able to do the following tasks with most readers: read articles, post articles, uudecode articles and subscribe/unsubscribe to groups. Let's take a quick look at some of these features.

When you choose to post an article, make sure your posting is well-written, clear, concise, spell-checked and doesn't ramble (sounds like the same rules we set up for e-mail messages). This is important so that folks who have to pay for their news connections don't pull down long and pointless postings.

Make sure that the posting is well-laid-out by keeping line lengths to 60 - 65 characters. Also if the message is long, you should state that fact by typing *long* in the subject area of the article.

Make sure that you don't post graphics or other binary files to a newsgroup that is text-based. There are groups that exist purely for binary types of files (remember binary files must be uuencoded). As long as we're discussing what not to post, don't post test messages to groups. If you absolutely, positively must do this, post to either *misc.test* or *alt.test* where you won't annoy anyone. You will receive an automatic e-mail reply if your test message was successful.

Finally, end your messages with a signature, if you want. Many news readers and e-mailers will allow you to create a signature file that will automatically be appended to anything that you post or send. This is a very convenient way to let others know your name and e-mail address. You should try to keep this signature to three or four lines long. My signature is:

```
----------------------------------------------------------------------
Scott D. James                                e-mail: sjames@nova.gmi.edu
Industrial & Manufacturing Systems Engineering
GMI Engineering & Management Institute        phone:(810) 762-9859
Flint, Michigan                               fax:  (810) 762-9924
```

Remember to keep your signature short; many groups won't accept postings with long signatures. A lot of users' signatures end with a humorous (but not obnoxious) saying or quote.

Watch out for anonymous postings. If your service provides the capability to do anonymous postings, you should seldom (if ever) use it. Why? If you want to say something, you should be brave enough to attach your name to it. Secondly, anonymous just means the message doesn't have your name or e-mail address in it; there is still a log of an incoming message from your site which could be traced should it become necessary to do so.

Cross-posting is another issue which you should be careful with. Cross-posting is sending a single article to multiple groups. Unfortunately some folks send articles to the wrong groups as well as to those that should receive them. If this is done knowingly, it's called "spamming." One example of a spam that circulates fairly regularly on most of the newgroups is the "get rich quick pyramid scheme."

Replying to a post is fairly easy as the news reader will fill in all the header information from the original article's header. Most readers will also include the original message. You should prune this down to just the important parts and then write your reply in.

An Example of Using UseNet News with a News Reader

The first thing that needs to be done is to start up a news reader. I use the *nn* reader which runs on my UNIX system. Most web browsers also provide support to read the news.

```
defiant{sjames}7% nn
Connecting to NNTP server zip.eecs.umich.edu ...
Connecting to NNTP server zip.eecs.umich.edu ... ok (posting is allowed)
Release 6.5b3.0 #6 (NOV), Kim F. Storm, 1991
```

Once *nn* is running, the first newsgroup which I read is shown. In this example it's *alt.3d*. You can also see that there are just over 1,000 articles to view in this newsgroup.

```
Reading alt.3d: 1025 articles
a  F X DeJesus       29  >>Chinalake WWW Site
b  F X DeJesus       13  >>MESHPAINT WHERE!!!!????
c  Dean Fogarty      13  Animation Master : any users ?
d  Juergen Fechter   15  >3DMAX View Star glasses
e  Neal G Thomas     10  >3d Model of Enterprise 1701d
f  Jack Campbell      8  New Low prices Print Posters 24x36 $12
g  SGiff68285         5  >Career as a special effects artist
h  James Fences       9  >3DS file formats
i  Dino Pannozzo      9  3D-Studio: does box-mapping also work for flat
j  Empty             14  >>>Product Info Needed
k  Jack Campbell     13  Poster from your pictures 24x36$12
l  Eric Klien        28  Oceania
m  giorgio natale     3  View Master
n  giorgio natale     3
o  giorgio natale     3  >3DS to Wavefront
p  Ben F M School     1  TEST
q  MT                 1  -
r  MT                 1  -

12:05 -- SELECT -- help:? -----Top 16%-----
```

I have been shown the first page of the 1,025 articles. I select whichever articles I want to read. I can then choose to read the articles immediately and return to the group to choose more, or I can finish choosing all of the articles that I want to see out of the 1,025 and view them all at once.

You should also notice that the last line of the screen shows that I can get help by pressing the ? character. The page of article subjects that I am viewing is the first 16% of the 1,025 articles. I can move from page to page by simply pressing the space bar. I select articles by typing the letter that precedes the article's author.

Let's select article *h* and immediately read it:

```
Sat, 8 Apr 95 17:51
>3DS file formats

>Does anyone have the file format that 3D studio uses?
You might want to see if AutoDesk has an ftp site.
Also, O'Reilly & Associates has a book called the Encyclopedia of
Computer Graphics Format or some such thing that probably has the
format.

Regards,
Jim
```

The article posted by Jim Fences is a reply to someone who apparently wanted to know about the format that AutoDesk's 3D Studio™ uses to save its files.

3.4 WRITING POSTINGS: A CHECKLIST

Here are a few suggestions that you might want to follow when posting messages to a newsgroup on the UseNet News:

- Make sure you are posting to the proper newsgroup(s).
- Make sure your posting has something to say in a concise manner, is spell-checked and uses proper English.
- People are not going to remember everything they have said. Paraphrase what you are replying to.
- If you are asking for help with a software program, make sure you tell what type of computer system it is running on and what version of the program you have.
- Don't post a message that says "when you reply, send e-mail, I don't read this group." If you have a question, chances are someone else has the same question. And, if you don't read the group, what are you doing posting on it?

3.5 ALTERNATE WAYS OF RECEIVING USENET NEWS

If you don't have access to a news reader there are a couple of other ways that you can get UseNet News. This section will examine these ways.

1) E-Mail. If you want, you can receive selected news through your e-mailer. This is sometimes advantageous since you might not have the time to run through a news reader. Stanford University has a news filtering service in which you can send an e-mail message requesting what you are looking for. The service will then scan the news and mail any related postings to you.

The address for this service is *netnews@db.stanford.edu* and the message body takes the following form:

subscribe <keywords>	the subject you're looking for—**subscribe 3D graphics**
period. <frequency>	how often you want to receive mail in days—**period 3**
[threshold <frequency>]	how well it has to relate to keywords (0 -100%)
[expire <frequency>]	when you want the service to stop in days

So if I wanted to have all articles that exactly match the criteria "computer graphics" bundled up and sent to me every 4 days and I want this service to stop in 12 days, I would send the following e-mail message:

```
defiant{sjames}8%mail netnews@db.stanford.edu
subscribe computer graphics
threshold 100
period 4
expire 12
```

Note: You can also check the *news.answers* newsgroup for more information on this service.

2) Gopher Some Gopher sites will carry partial UseNet News: *info.latech.edu, pinchy.micro.umn.edu and src.doc.ic.ac.uk.* The advantage to using Gopher is that there are several public Gopher sites which are available versus few public news server sites. The disadvantages of using Gopher to read the news include the fact that most Gopher sites do not allow posting capabilities and most have limited threading capabilities. Gophers will be discussed in Chapter 5.

3) Web Browsers Most web browsers will allow you to specify an NNTP_Server (news server) in their configuration. Once this is done, you can usually specify the news group name in the URL space following the format of *news:newsgroup.* See Chapter 6 for more information on web browsers and URLs.

Chapter Summary

This chapter looked at the original mass media communications available on the Internet: mailing lists and UseNet News. The chapter provided coverage of how to subscribe, unsubscribe and post to both LISTSERV and Majordomo type mailing lists. The chapter then examined UseNet newsgroups and the common tasks performed with them. The chapter concluded with an examination of alternative ways of getting the UseNet News without a newsreader.

Key Terms

Digested
LISTSERV
Mailing Lists

Majordomo
Moderated
newsgroup
newsreader
Signature File
Subscribing
Undigested
Unmoderated
Unsubscribing
UseNet News

PROBLEMS

1. Try subscribing to a mailing list. You can either get a copy of the news.lists directory or try one from the following list:

   CAD Mailing List:

   List Address: *cadam-l@suvm.syr.edu*

   Subscription Address: *listserv@suvm.syr.edu*

   History Mailing List:

   List Address: *hist-l@rutvm1.rutgers.edu*

   Subscription Address: *listserv@rutvm1.rutgers.edu*

   Net Happenings List:

   List Address: *net-happenings@is.internic.net*

   Subscription Address: *listserv@is.internic.net*

2. Print out your subscription notification e-mail message. You can then unsubscribe from the list if you want.
3. Use your newsreader to join a newsgroup. Print out any article that you thought was interesting from that newsgroup.

CHAPTER

4

Telnet, FTP & Locating Files

SCIENCE/ENGINEERING SPOTLIGHT: NANOTECHNOLOGY

Imagine someone having a heart attack and the hospital personnel are able to determine the extent of the damage and repair it without performing a catheterization. Even though it sounds like sci-fi, the possibility is on the horizon with nanotechnology. Nanotechnology is the creation of extremely minute machines that can have motors, tools and computers built into them. In the above scenario, the hospital personnel could inject a nano-machine, with a microscopic video camera and perhaps a laser, into the patient's blood stream. The video camera could send back images of the heart damage, while the laser could remove the plaque which caused the heart attack from the artery walls. After the nano-machine has done its work, it could either be removed from some predetermined point or left in the blood stream and purged by the body.

Objectives

This chapter begins by examining how to access computers around the Internet via the Telnet program. The second portion of the chapter explains the process of FTP, which is a program used to retrieve files. A brief examination of the different file types found on the Internet is then provided. The chapter concludes with a look at finding specific files on the Internet via the Archie program.

4.1 TELNET

Telnet is a program that lets you connect (log in) to a remote computer over the Internet. Once you have connected to the remote computer, you can use any resources that are available on that remote computer just as if you were accessing the resource locally.

Telnet comes in very handy if you are traveling and need access to your computer at home, work, or school. You simply hook locally into the Internet and use Telnet to make the connection to your remote computer. Another nice feature of Telnet is that you can connect to several remote computers at the same time (or the same computer multiple times) and do work simultaneously.

Telnet is a text-based program. You aren't going to see any neat graphics or fancy interfaces. You may be asked to specify a terminal type. The common types are ANSI, TTY and VT100. ANSI supports color; TTY is a very plain terminal; VT100 is an old DEC terminal type and is probably both the most common and widely used choice.

How Do I Telnet?

Telnet is available on most computers. The basic usage of it is to type:

```
Telnet hostname [port]
```

— or —

```
Telnet IPaddress [port]
```

When using Telnet, you can use either the hostname or the IP address since they both equate to the same computer. After you have entered this command, Telnet will try to connect to the remote computer. If it is successful, you will be prompted for your username and password.

Occasionally you may need to specify a port number. Most of the time we just type the Telnet command which connects us to the Telnet port on the remote computer. The Telnet port allows us to log in to the computer. There are instances when we don't want to connect to the Telnet port, but rather to a specific port. That's when we would supply the port number after the hostname or IP address. An example of this was seen in Chapter 2 when we Telneted to the KIS server at Reston. The command was `telnet nri.reston.va.us 185`. The 185 is a port which, when attached to, supplies us with the Knowbot Information Service (KIS).

Telnet may not always be able to make the connection that you request. There are primarily three reasons that you might not be able to get to the host you specified:

- you misspelled the hostname
- the host computer is down
- the host computer is not connected to the Internet

The second method to accessing Telnet is to just type the command `Telnet`. You will then receive a `Telnet>` prompt from where you can issue the following Telnet commands:

`?`	print help information
`close`	stop communications with the remote computer
`display`	display operating parameters
`mode`	try to enter line-by-line or character-by-character mode
`open` *host*	attempt to start communications with a remote computer
`quit`	end the Telnet program
`send`	transmit special characters ('send ?' for more)
`set`	set operating parameters ('set ?' for more)
`status`	print status information
`toggle`	toggle operating parameters ('toggle ?' for more)
`z`	suspend Telnet

You also should be aware of the CTRL-] key. This keystroke interrupts your session with the remote computer and returns you to the `Telnet>` prompt. At that point, you can issue the `quit` command to stop communications with the remote computer and end your Telnet session.

An Example of Using Telnet

In this example, I am going to log in to a computer that is physically housed two floors below the computer I am currently using. I could just as easily be accessing a computer halfway around the world.

```
defiant{sjames}10% Telnet markviii.cimlab.gmi.edu
Trying 192.138.137.41 ...
Connected to markviii.cimlab.gmi.edu.
Escape character is '^]'.
```

At this point I have made the connection, and can now attempt to enter my username and password to log in to the computer.

```
************************************************************************
*   Unauthorized Access to this computer system or any information    *
*         contained therein is a violation of federal law.            *
************************************************************************

SunOS UNIX (markviii)
login: sjames
Password:
Last login: Tue May 23 09:46:22 from nova.gmi.edu
SunOS Release 4.1.3_U1 (MARKVIII) #1: Fri Oct 21 16:34:40 EDT 1994
You have new mail.
```

I am remotely connected to the computer and can issue any command which could be issued if I was actually sitting at the computer.

```
markviii{sjames}1% from
From aleonard Thu Apr 27 13:11:12 1996
From cjames Tue May 16 18:13:18 1996
From hjames Wed May 17 12:01:23 1996

markviii{sjames}2% lpr -Pcimsparc todolist.txt
```

Notice that the last command is a UNIX command which will print out a file. I can now walk downstairs and I would find that my printout went to the remote printer that I specified. The nice thing about this is that I could do this from my office at work, my office at home or anywhere else in the world on the Internet!

Some Telnet Sites to Practice with

If you don't have a remote computer to Telnet to, here are a few places on the Internet to try. Notice that some of the names also need a port number. If a username is required, it is put in parentheses.

access.usask.ca (hytelnet)	Online libraries
astro.temple.edu 12345	Quotation cookie server
columbia.ilc.com (cas)	CDs, videotapes and software
cs.indiana.edu 2627 (webster)	Online Webster's dictionary
culine.colorado.edu 862	Today's baseball schedule
downwind.sprl.umich.edu 3000	Weather information
fdabbs.fda.gov (bbs)	FDA database
fedix.fie.com (fedix)	Federal hiring information
fedix.fie.com (molis)	Minority college information
glis.cr.usgs.gov (guest)	Global land usage
hpcvbbs.cv.hp.com	HP calculators
india.colorado.edu 13	MST from an atomic clock
locis.loc.gov	Library of Congress
martini.eecs.umich.edu 3000	Geographic information

pac.carl.org	Colorado Alliance of Research Libraries
ucsdbkst.ucsd.edu	U of C at San Diego's bookstore

Although it's not a site to practice with, you can get to CompuServe over the Internet by Telneting to *compuserve.com*. When you see the hostname prompt, type CIS. You will then get a short disclaimer on usage of CompuServe (or you can type CIS-AGREE to avoid the disclaimer). You can then type `logon` and select the baud rate (remember the higher the baud rate, the faster the data flow & the more dollars you pay to CompuServe). Finally you will be prompted for your CompuServe User ID and password.

Practice!

Let's practice our Telnet skills by finding out the population for Flint, Michigan. To do this, I can Telnet to the geographic information database that is stored at *martini.eecs.umich.edu 3000*. Let's see it happen (the bold text indicates what I typed):

```
telnet martini.eecs.umich.edu 3000
Trying 141.213.11.44 ...
Connected to martini . eecs.umich.edu.
Escape character is '^]'.
# Geographic Name Server, Copyright 1992 Regents of the University of Michigan.
# Version 8/19/92.  Use "help" or "?" for assistance, "info" for hints.
.
```

The easiest way to use this system is to simply type the zip code of the location you are interested in. If you want the full set of instructions, type `help` or ?.

```
48504
0 Northwest
1 26049 Genesee
2 MI Michigan
3 US United States
F 45 Populated place
Z 48504 48531 48532

0 Flint
1 26049 Genesee
2 MI Michigan
3 US United States
R county seat
F 45 Populated place
L 43 00 45 N  83 41 15 W
P 159611
E 712
Z 48500 48501 48502 48503 48504 48505 48506 48507 48508 48509
Z 48529 48531 48532 48550 48551 48552 48553 48554 48555 48556
Z 48559
```

From the information returned, you can see that the population "P" is 159,611. I can now type quit to leave the system since I have the information that I was looking for. Try it for your city!

4.2 ALTERNATIVE WAYS OF TELNETING

What happens when you need to Telnet to some site that interests you, but you don't have Telnet access locally?

1) Gopher Many times when you are using Gopher, you will be given a message that contains the hostname and/or IP address of the computer you are connecting to. You should write this information down. That way you can Telnet directly to the host without having to go through the Gopher menus every time. You should know that some of the support that Gopher supplies is in the form of a Telnet session, therefore, Gopher has the Telnet service built in.

In the future then, you can start Gopher with the address of the computer you want to Telnet to, thus gaining access. Gopher is examined in Chapter 5.

2) Web Browsers Most web browsers allow you to perform a Telnet session by typing `telnet://hostname` in the browser's URL line. Web browsers are examined in Chapter 6.

4.3 FTP

FTP stands for File Transfer Protocol and is simply what it says: a mechanism for transferring files between two computers. FTP (and Telnet) is one of the oldest TCP/IP protocols around. It's very simple to use and effective in what it does. FTP will allow you to transfer both binary and text files. One warning is necessary; FTP is case-sensitive when it comes to working with both files and commands.

Why use FTP?

- It's a quick and painless way to transfer files from home to work or school and vice versa.
- You may encounter a data file somewhere on the Internet that you would like to bring into your own computer.
- There is enough free software on the Internet to last a lifetime for every computer system imaginable. A list of publicly accessible FTP sites is available by anonymous FTP from *pilot.njin.net* in the */pub/ftp-list/* directory.

How Do I Use FTP?

Because FTP and Telnet are old TCP/IP programs, both have the same operating mechanics. We can start an FTP session by typing:

```
ftp hostname
```

— or —

```
ftp IPaddress
```

— or —

`ftp` (which will get you an `ftp>` prompt, then)

```
open host
```

In any event, FTP will attempt to connect you to the specified host. If it is successful, you will be prompted to log in. If the computer you have FTP-ed to is a private FTP server, you will probably need to have an account on that computer in order to access it. If the FTP server is a public server, you can usually log in by supplying *anonymous* for the username and your full electronic address for the password.

If you can't connect to a given FTP site, and the FTP server is a public server, you may be shown a list of mirror sites that you could try to FTP to. A mirror site is a site that carries an exact copy of what is on the computer you were trying to reach.

The FTP commands that you typically use during a session are:

ascii	States you are going to perform an access in text mode
bin	States you are going to perform an access in binary mode
bye	Logs out of the FTP computer
cd	Changes directory on the FTP computer
dir	Lists files, but with more information, such as size, date created, etc.
get ***file***	Downloads the file from the FTP computer to your computer
hash	Displays # marks while files are being transferred
help	Gives a list of commands
lcd	Change directory on the local machine
ls	Lists files in the current directory
mget ***file***	Used to get multiple files
mput ***file***	Used to put multiple files
prompt	Toggles prompt mode for `mget` or `mput` operations
put ***file***	Uploads the file from your computer to the FTP computer

Note: `get` and `mget` will automatically overwrite any local files with the same name!

An Example Use of FTP

In this example, I am going to FTP to a computer at Oakland University located in Rochester, Michigan and download a copy of the MS-DOS anti-virus package F-PROT. I begin by invoking the FTP command with the computer that I want to connect to at Oakland.

```
nova{sjames}5% ftp oak.oakland.edu
Connected to oak.oakland.edu.
220 oak.oakland.edu FTP server (Version wu-2.4(9) Wed May 3 15:02:49 EDT
1995) ready.
```

At this point, I am connected to the computer at Oakland and my username and password will be requested. I will type in *anonymous* for the username and *sjames@defiant.gmi.edu* for the password. Since Oakland is a public FTP site, this will work just fine.

```
Name (oak.oakland.edu:sjames): anonymous
331 Guest login ok, send your complete e-mail address as password.
Password:
230-
230-                    Welcome to
230-               THE OAK SOFTWARE REPOSITORY
230-      A service of Oakland University, Rochester Michigan
230-
230- If you have trouble using OAK with your ftp client, please try
using
230- a dash (-) as the first character of your password — this will turn
230- off the continuation messages that may be confusing your ftp
client.
230- OAK is a Unix machine, and filenames are case sensitive.
230-
230- Access is allowed at any time.  If you have any unusual problems,
230- please report them via electronic mail to archives@Oakland.Edu
230-
230- You are user #329 out of 400 maximum users on Wed May 24 12:14:28
1995.
230-
230- Oak is also on the World Wide Web, URL:
http://www.acs.oakland.edu/oak.html
230-
230- File searching is now available!  Example command:  site exec index
4dos
230-
230-Please read the file README
230-  it was last modified on Fri Mar 24 18:59:19 1995 - 61 days ago
230 Guest login ok, access restrictions apply.
```

I'm now logged into the computer. Let's take a look around:

```
ftp> dir
200 PORT command successful.
150 Opening ASCII mode data connection for /bin/ls.
total 1258
-rw-r--r--   1 w8sdz    OAK             0 Nov 13  1994 .notar
drwxr-x---   2 root     operator     8192 Dec 31 16:44 .quotas
drwx------   2 root     system       8192 Dec 30 19:16 .tags
-rw-r--r--   1 jeff     OAK       1093470 May 24 03:20 Index-byname
-r--r--r--   1 w8sdz    OAK          1237 Mar 24 18:59 README
drwxr-xr-x   3 w8sdz    OAK          8192 May 19 17:53 SimTel
d--x--x--x   3 root     system       8192 Jan 19 20:26 bin
d--x--x--x   2 root     system       8192 Jul 30  1994 core
drwxr-x---   2 cpm      OAK          8192 Nov 21  1994 cpm-incoming
d--x--x--x   5 root     system       8192 Dec 30 05:15 etc
```

```
drwxrwx---   2 incoming OAK          8192 May 24 11:54 incoming
drwxrwx---   2 25913    OAK          8192 Apr 23 10:50 nt-incoming
drwxr-xr-x   3 w8sdz    OAK          8192 Apr 13 19:46 pub
drwxr-xr-x  15 w8sdz    OAK          8192 Apr 13 19:46 pub2
drwxr-xr-x   8 w8sdz    OAK          8192 May  3 13:24 pub3
drwxr-xr-x   3 w8sdz    OAK          8192 May 19 17:53 simtel
drwxr-xr-x   2 jeff     OAK          8192 Apr 17  1994 siteinfo
drwx------  46 w8sdz    OAK          8192 May 22 21:42 w8sdz
226 Transfer complete.
1133 bytes received in 0.45 seconds (2.5 Kbytes/s)
```

I happen to know that the MS-DOS programs are located in the SimTel directory, so let's change directories.

```
ftp> cd SimTel
250-The files in this directory tree are a mirror of SimTel, the Coast
to
250-Coast Software Repository (tm).  Please read README.COPYRIGHT for
250-information on distribution rights.
250-
250-Please read the file README.COPYRIGHT
250-  it was last modified on Sun Apr 23 01:32:42 1995 - 31 days ago
250-Please read the file README.MIRRORING
250-  it was last modified on Thu Apr 27 12:49:22 1995 - 27 days ago
250 CWD command successful.
```

There's the msdos directory. Let's change there:

```
ftp> dir
200 PORT command successful.
150 Opening ASCII mode data connection for /bin/ls.
total 32
-rw-r--r--   1 w8sdz    OAK           172 Jan 28 15:05 .message
-rw-r--r--   1 w8sdz    OAK             0 Jan 28 15:05 .notar
-rw-r--r--   3 w8sdz    OAK          4605 Apr 23 01:32 README.COPYRIGHT
-rw-r--r--   3 w8sdz    OAK          1632 Apr 27 12:49 README.MIRRORING
drwxr-xr-x 221 w8sdz    OAK          8192 May 22 01:27 msdos
drwxr-xr-x  11 djgruber OAK          8192 May 20 02:57 nt
drwxr-xr-x  84 w8sdz    OAK          8192 May 23 23:21 win3
226 Transfer complete.
459 bytes received in 0.011 seconds (41 Kbytes/s)
ftp> cd msdos
250-This MS-DOS collection is a mirror of SimTel, the Coast to Coast
250-Software Repository (tm).  Questions about or comments on this
250-collection should be sent to w8sdz@SimTel.Coast.NET.
250-
250-Please read the file README.COPYRIGHT
250-  it was last modified on Sun Apr 23 01:32:42 1995 - 31 days ago
250-Please read the file README.MIRRORING
```

```
250-  it was last modified on Thu Apr 27 12:49:22 1995 - 27 days ago
250-Please read the file README.descriptions
250-  it was last modified on Sun Apr 23 01:38:53 1995 - 31 days ago
250-Please read the file README.dir-list
250-  it was last modified on Mon May 22 01:24:32 1995 - 2 days ago
250-Please read the file README.file-formats
250-  it was last modified on Sun Apr 23 01:40:24 1995 - 31 days ago
250-Please read the file README.how-to-upload
250-  it was last modified on Sun Apr 23 01:35:51 1995 - 31 days ago
250-Please read the file README.simtel-cdrom
250-  it was last modified on Fri May 12 12:36:58 1995 - 12 days ago
250 CWD command successful.
```

The msdos directory is huge; it probably has a couple hundred subdirectories. I know the name of the subdirectory that I'm looking for is virus. Let's change to that subdirectory.

```
ftp> cd virus
250 CWD command successful.
```

Let's look for any files that start with fp:

```
ftp> dir fp*.*
200 PORT command successful.
150 Opening ASCII mode data connection for /bin/ls.
-rw-r--r--   1 w8sdz    OAK       564320 Apr  2 16:04 fp-217.zip
226 Transfer complete.
remote: fp*.*
66 bytes received in 0.0051 seconds (13 Kbytes/s)
```

There's the file we're interested in. It's a binary file; I'll explain how I know in a minute. Change into binary mode and download the file.

```
ftp> bin
200 Type set to I.
ftp> get fp-217.zip
200 PORT command successful.
150 Opening BINARY mode data connection for fp-217.zip (564320 bytes).
226 Transfer complete.
local: fp-217.zip remote: fp-217.zip
564320 bytes received in 92 seconds (6 Kbytes/s)
```

I just downloaded one-half meg in 92 seconds. I now have a copy of the F-PROT program on my computer and I can do what I want with it. Since I'm all finished, I'll stop the FTP program.

```
ftp> quit
221 Goodbye.
```

Sample FTP Sites to Start with

ames.arc.nasa.gov	NASA files & images
atari.archive.umich.edu	Atari files
cathouse.org	Entertainment Information
explorer.arc.nasa.gov	NASA Explorer
ftp.cica.indiana.edu	Windows software
ftp.fedworld.gov	Helps you find federal government documents
ftp.microsoft.com	Microsoft's FTP site
ftp.ncsa.uiuc.edu	Incomplete Guide to the Internet
ftp.near.net	Commerce Business Daily
ftp.product.com	Provider of product information
ftp.senate.gov	U.S. Senate
ftp.utas.edu.au	Home of the Trumpet software packages
ftp.uu.net	Amiga & Mac files
marvel.loc.gov	Library of Congress
mrcnext.cso.uiuc.edu	Project Gutenberg
oak.oakland.edu	A SimTel site with a lot of everything
stats.bls.gov	Bureau of Labor Statistics
sunsite.unc.edu	Internet tools and Sun information
wiretap.spies.com	FOIA home with lots of information
wuarchive.wustl.edu	Washington University at St. Louis site SimTel mirror

PRACTICE!

Let's try to FTP the file called README from the FTP site *oak.oakland.edu*. You will need to connect as user *anonymous* and type your username for the password. The bold text indicates what I typed.

```
ftp oak.oakland.edu
Connected to oak.oakland.edu.
220 oak.oakland.edu FTP server (Version wu-2.4(9) Wed May 3 15:02:49 EDT
1995) r
eady.
Name (oak.oakland.edu:sjames): anonymous
331 Guest login ok, send your complete e-mail address as password.
Password:
230-
230-                          Welcome to
230-                     THE OAK SOFTWARE REPOSITORY
230-          A service of Oakland University, Rochester Michigan
230-
230- If you have trouble using OAK with your ftp client, please try
using
230- a dash (-) as the first character of your password — this will turn
230- off the continuation messages that may be confusing your ftp
client.
```

```
230- OAK is a Unix machine, and filenames are case sensitive.
230-
230- Access is allowed at any time.  If you have any unusual problems,
230- please report them via electronic mail to archives@Oakland.Edu
230-
230- Oak is also on the World Wide Web, URL: http://oak.oakland.edu/
230-
230- To search for files, use the command: quote site exec index file-
name
230-
230-Please read the file README
230-  it was last modified on Fri Mar 22 15:07:51 1996 - 146 days ago
230 Guest login ok, access restrictions apply.
```

Now that we're on the system, let's look around:

```
ftp>dir
200 PORT command successful.
150 Opening ASCII mode data connection for /bin/ls.
total 1874
-rw-r--r--   1 w8sdz    OAK            0 Nov 13  1994 .notar
drwxr-x---   2 root     operator    8192 Dec 31  1994 .quotas
drwx------   2 root     system      8192 Dec 30  1994 .tags
-rw-r--r--   1 jeff     OAK      1826389 Aug 15 03:19 Index-byname
-r--r--r--   1 w8sdz    OAK         1386 Mar 22 15:07 README
drwxr-xr-x   2 jeff     OAK         8192 Apr 28 22:21 SimTel
d--x--x--x   3 root     system      8192 Jan 19  1995 bin
d--x--x--x   2 root     system      8192 May  6 16:11 core
drwxr-x---   3 cpm      OAK         8192 Mar 22 16:46 cpm-incoming
d--x--x--x   6 root     system      8192 Aug 14 03:14 etc
drwxr-xr-x  10 jeff     OAK         8192 Jul 22 08:32 irc
drwxr-xr-x  16 w8sdz    OAK         8192 Jul 24 15:41 pub
drwxr-xr-x   2 jeff     OAK         8192 Apr 17  1994 siteinfo
drwx------  46 w8sdz    OAK         8192 Aug  5 19:48 w8sdz
226 Transfer complete.
879 bytes received in 0.13 seconds (6.6 Kbytes/s)
```

Since we see the file README, let's get it:

```
ftp>get README
200 PORT command successful.
150 Opening ASCII mode data connection for README (1386 bytes).
226 Transfer complete.
local: README remote: README
1415 bytes received in 0.17 seconds (8 Kbytes/s)
```

Now that we've received it, let's type `quit` to stop the FTP program.

```
ftp> quit
221 Goodbye.
```

If you look at your local disk now, you should see that you have a copy of the README file on it.

4.4 WHAT DO ALL THE FILE EXTENSIONS MEAN?

Most of the time when we are accessing binary files via FTP they are somehow compressed or archived. This really isn't anything that we need to be alarmed about, we just need to know what to uncompress or unarchive the files with. This section is designed to point out the common file extensions and the program that produced them. If you are trying to download a file in the binary files section, make sure that you type the `bin` command before you try to *get* the file. This is the reason that I knew to use `bin` when I brought down the F-PROT package in the previous example.

BINARY FILES

.au	Sun Audio files
.bmp	Graphics/Image files
.com	PC executables (programs)
.exe	PC executables (programs)
.gif	Graphics/Image files
.gl	Graphics/Image files
.gz	GNU ZIP file. Use gunzip or gzip -d to extract the files
.hqx	Macintosh BINHEX file. Use unhqx to extract the files (unmacit.zip)
.jpg	Graphics/Image files
.lha	LH archive. Use lharc to extract the files
.mpg	Graphics/Image files
.pcx	Graphics/Image files
.qt	Macintosh QuickTime movie format
.shar	Shell archive. Use unshar to extract the files
.sit	Macintosh StuffIt format. Use unstuffit to extract the files
.tar	UNIX tape archive file. Use tar -xvf to extract the files
.tif	Graphics/Image files
.wav	Windows Audio files
.Z or .z	UNIX compress file. Use uncompress to extract the files
.zip	ZIP file. Use pkunzip to unzip the files
.zoo	ZOO archive. Use zoo -extract to extract the files

TEXT FILES

.me	Readme files
.ps	Postscript files
.txt	Text files
.uue	UUEncoded files

When you are FTP-ing you should always start looking at files called README, INDEX and so forth. These files will give you information about what may be contained in a directory. You can usually view a text file directly on the screen by issuing the command `get` *`filename`* `|more`. There should be no space between the | and the command *`more`*.

If you download a file that has been compressed, you will need to uncompress it before you can use it. Many sites that you FTP to will have a directory which contains the appropriate program to uncompress the files. You may need to look around a bit, but you can find the files.

4.5 ALTERNATIVE WAYS OF FTP-ING

This section addresses ways to FTP files using e-mail when you don't have FTP access. One site that e-mails files to you is *ftpmail.decwrl.dec.com*. To perform the FTP via e-mail, send a message to the server and put the FTP commands in the body of the message which you would have to type if you were manually FTP-ing. Valid FTP commands include: `ASCII, binary, get, dir, ls, help, quit.`

```
– and –

reply yourfulladdress          where to mail the files
connect host                   the host where the files are
chdir                          change directory
```

An example of using this method is:

```
To:  ftpmail@decwrl.dec.com
Subject:
Message:  reply sjames@nova.gmi.edu
          connect oak.oakland.edu
          chdir /SimTel/msdos/virus
          get fp-217.zip
          quit
```

If the file that you requested is larger than 64K, *ftpmail* will break it up into several numbered sections that you will have to put back together using your computer's particular operating system.

Here's a list of the other *ftpmail* servers around the world:

ftpmail@grasp.insa-lyon.fr	134.214.100.25	France
bitftp@vm.grd.de	192.88.97.13	German
ftpmail@ieunet.ie	192.111.39.1	Ireland
ftpmail@decwrl.dec.com	16.1.0.1	USA: California
bitftp@pucc.princeton.edu	128.112.129.99	USA: New Jersey

4.6 HOW CAN I FIND FILES?

Locating files on the Internet that can be obtained through FTP is made possible through a program known as Archie. Archie is accessible in three different ways:

1) you can Telnet to an Archie server
2) you could have your own Archie program

3) you could e-mail an Archie server with a query, with the server e-mailing its results back to you.

Let's examine each of these.

We could begin by Telneting to *archie.rutgers.edu* and logging in with a username of `archie`; no password is required. A list of public Archie servers is provided at the end of this chapter.

You will now receive an `archie>` prompt. At this point you can enter search commands; `help` will provide help and `quit` will end using the server.

The next step that we should perform is to set our search variables. The command `show` will show what all variables are currently set at. You can also type `show variable` to find out the value of a particular variable. Let's look at these variables and their associated values:

ENVIRONMENT VARIABLES

`set pager` [on | off]	You should set pager to `on` if you want Archie to display its search results to your screen. It causes the results to pause after a pageful has been displayed.
`set status` [on | off]	Set status to `on` if you want Archie to display a status line at the bottom of the screen as it searches.
`set autologout` [x]	This value controls how many minutes Archie will wait for you to enter a command without logging you off (range is 1 - 300).
`set maxhits` [x]	This value tells Archie that if it finds the same file *x* times to stop searching (start at 10 and move up as needed).
`set mailto` *fullusername*	If you want Archie to mail its results to you, you should set this variable to your *username@host* information.

OUTPUT DENSITY VARIABLES

`set output_format verbose`	Give as much information as possible
`set output_format terse`	Give basic information
`set output_format machine`	Used to specify a program to manipulate the mailed output

SORTING VARIABLES

`set sortby none`	Do not sort
`set sortby filename`	Sort alphabetical by filename
`set sortby hostname`	Sort alphabetical by hostname
`set sortby size`	Sort largest to smallest
`set sortby time`	Sort newest to oldest
`set sortby rfilename`	Reverse sort alphabetical by filename
`set sortby rhostname`	Reverse sort alphabetical by hostname

`set sortby rsize`	Sort smallest to largest
`set sortby rtime`	Sort oldest to newest

SEARCHING VARIABLES

`set search exact`	Find IBM-PC matches IBM-PC but not IBM-pc or ibm-pc
`set search sub`	Find PC matches IBM-PC, PC or pc-DOS
`set search subcase`	Find PC matches IBM-PC but not pc-DOS
`set search regex`	UNIX regular expression such that PC$ would find anything ending with the letters PC
`set search exact_sub`	Try exact then try search sub
`set search exact_subcase`	Try exact then try search subcase
`set search exact_regex`	Try exact then try search regex

METACHARACTERS:

The main regular expression metacharacters for use in regex are:
`$` - indicates ending with; `PC$` would find anything ending with PC
`^` - indicated beginning with; `^pkunzip` would find anything starting with pkunzip
`.` - match any character
`*` - match zero or more preceding
`[ ]` - match one from a set

EXAMPLES OF METACHARACTER MATCHES:

Pattern	**What does it match?**
bag	bag
^bag	bag, baggage
bag$	old-bag
^bag$	bag
[Bb]ag	Bag, bag
b[aeiou]g	bag, beg, big, bog, bug
b.g	b anything for the second character g
^...$	any line with exactly three characters
bugs*	bug, bugs ,bugss, etc.
"word"	a word in quotes
"*word"*	a word with or without quotes

The last command that we need to supply is `find` which tells Archie to look for a file with the supplied name. In older versions of Archie this command was called `prog`.

A Sample Archie Search:

```
Archie> set maxhits 10
Archie> set output_format verbose
Archie> set pager
Archie> set search exact_sub
Archie> set sortby time
```

```
Archie> set status
Archie> find fp-217.zip
```

Archie would now start up and try to locate the file *fp-217.zip*. If you want Archie to stop before it finishes searching, press the CTRL-C combination. Once Archie has completed a search, you can e-mail the results to yourself by entering the command `mail` given that you have set the `mailto` variable. Otherwise you must type `mail yourfulladdress`. So in the example, I started above, I could type the following command to mail my results as soon as I get the `Archie>` prompt back:

```
Archie> mail sjames@defiant.gmi.edu
```

Once the results are displayed on your screen there are a few keystrokes which are convenient to know when looking at the output. The space bar moves forward one full screen; `q` quits the output; `b` goes backward one screen; `/pattern` says to search forward for the given pattern (you can use `?pattern` to search backwards); and `n` will repeat the previous search.

The `find` command works great if you know the name of a file, but what if you only know part of the name or worse yet, none of it? This is the purpose of the `whatis` command. You simply type `whatis itemtosearchfor` and `whatis` will return anything with a description containing that item. The only limitation on `whatis` is that the person who submitted the file to the Archie database needed to supply a description that contains your search word in it.

Finally a word on Archie help. `Help ?` brings up a list of all commands and `help command` brings up detailed help on the specified command. The same keystrokes mentioned above for viewing the Archie output will work with help too.

The second way that you may be able to access Archie is on your local computer. Try typing `archie` and see if you get the `archie>` prompt. The way this version of Archie works is a little different from Telneting to an Archie server. You won't need to set variables as in the example above, and the entire command will fit on one line. For example `archie -m10 -s fp-217.zip` tells the computer to set the maxhits to 10 and using a sub search look for the file `fp-217.zip` with the output going to your screen. All the commands are typically switches that are supplied on the command line and documented below:

`-c`	set search subcase
`-e`	set search exact
`-h`*address*	send Archie server requests to the specified host
`-l`	set output_format machine
`-L`	show list of known Archie servers
`-m`*number*	set maxhits
`-o`*filename*	send the output to the specified file
`-r`	set search regex
`-s`	set search sub
`-t`	set sortby time
`-V`	make comment during a long search

Finally, you can search Archie through e-mail by sending a message to *archie@archie.internic.net* or *archie@archie.mcgill.ca.* You simply type a text message with each of the variables and commands that you would normally type if you were performing an Archie search via a Telnet session.

If you would like to receive information on how to use the Archie e-mail service, send a message with `help` as the body.

```
To:       archie@archie.internic.net
Subject:
Message:  set mailto sjames@nova.gmi.edu
          set maxhits 25
          set output_format verbose
          set search exact
          set sortby time
          find fp-217.zip
          quit
```

List of Publicly Available Archie Servers in the U.S. and Canada

archie.uqam.ca	Canada
archie.mcgill.ca	Canada
archie.sura.net	U.S.:Maryland
archie.unl.edu	U.S.:Nebraska
archie.internic.net	U.S.:New Jersey
archie.rutgers.edu	U.S.:New Jersey
archie.ans.net	U.S.:New York

Chapter Summary

This chapter looked at two of the oldest communications programs around: Telnet and FTP. Telnet provides users with the ability to log on to computers located around the Internet. FTP is a program which allows users to copy files from some remote computer to their own local computer. The chapter concluded with an examination of how to locate specific filenames on the Internet.

Key Terms

Archie
Archive
Binary Files
Compressed
FTP
Port
Telnet
Text Files

PROBLEMS

1. Practice Telneting to computers that are located on your school's campus.
2. Telnet to *downwind.sprl.umich.edu 3000* and print out the weather forecast for your vicinity.
3. Telnet to *martini.eecs.umich.edu 3000* and print out the geographic information for your home town (remember to use your zip code).
4. Retrieve a text file via FTP from a computer of your instructor's choice. Print that file out.
5. FTP the latest version of the MS-DOS anti-virus package F-PROT. You can get it from the */pub/simtelnet/msdos/virus* directory at *oak.oakland.edu*.
6. Use an ARCHIE server to find other Internet sites where the latest version of F-PROT can be found. Print this list out.

CHAPTER 5

Gopher & WAIS

SCIENCE/ENGINEERING SPOTLIGHT: VIRTUAL REALITY

We've all seen the games in the malls, where contestants put on headsets and gloves and try to "zap" each other with lasers while avoiding being a pterodactyl snack. We've also seen movies like *Lawnmower Man* and *Virtuosity* which depict virtual worlds. Where does virtual reality currently exist though? Virtual reality is still in its infancy, in which most participants must wear some kind of goggles or headset in order to see and hear the virtual world. If one wants to manipulate items in the virtual world, some kind of special glove apparatus is required. We are making advances in trying to allow people to become more immersed in the technology through special suits that provide tactile feedback. The truth of the matter is that we are still a long way from what movies show VR as being.

OBJECTIVES

This chapter examines the last two of the text-based services on the Internet. Gophers are a menu-driven approach to integrating the collection of data resources pooled through Telneting and FTP-ing. Gopher is actually a forerunner to the web browsers which will be examined in Chapter 6. WAIS is a collection of databases which users can select to perform searches on. Any matches found in the databases can be immediately retrieved from the WAIS interface.

5.1 GOPHER

As you have seen from the preceding Internet services that we have discussed, we have used different programs to perform different tasks. Gopher integrates these different tasks into a common text-based environment. Gopher is a menu-driven system that allows access to different resources as needed at sites across the Internet. You don't even need to know exactly where something is stored before you try to find it. You will just set your Gopher software to point at some Gopher server and you're all set. The bottom line to Gopher is that if you can use a table of contents in a book, you can jump all over the Internet retrieving the kinds of information that you want.

Gopher-Related Terms

The following is a list of terms that are commonly referred to when using a Gopher:

- Document: The actual object associated with an item. It is usually text, but objects can come in other forms.
- Gopherspace: The total of all Gopher resources on the Internet.
- Item: Any item that appears on a menu: it could be another menu, a directory, document or search that appears on a menu.
- Server: A computer system that provides the Gopher's menus and stores the related documents.

How Do I Use Gopher?

You must have some form of Gopher software available to you, then simply point that software at a Gopher server. Everything is menu-driven. Gopher software is truly client/server in nature. The client portion is the program that resides on your computer and the server portion is the actual documents and menus which exist on Gopher servers.

The newer versions of Gopher are starting to blur with the World Wide Web in that Gopher is no longer exclusively text. Audio files, graphic images and animations are just a few of the documents that are retrievable and viewable with the newer versions of Gopher software.

An Example of Using Gopher

I begin this example by starting the local Gopher program loaded on my computer at GMI.

```
nova{sjames}4% gopher
Welcome to the wonderful world of Gopher!

Gopher has limitations on its use and comes without
a warranty. Please refer to the file 'Copyright' included
in the distribution.

Internet Gopher Information Client 2.0 patch16
Copyright 1991,92,93,94 by the Regents of the University of Minnesota

Press RETURN to continue
```

Gopher has now started; pressing the return key brings up the main menu.

```
GMI Gopher Information Server Main Menu

 --> 1.  About This Gopher at GMI(Updated 3/5/95)
     2.  The GMI Undergraduate Catalog - 1994-1995 <HTML>
     3.  Academic Programs/
     4.  CSO Version of the GMI Phonebook <CSO>
     5.  Unix Update - GMI/
     6.  Calendars and Schedules/
     7.  Computer Policy at GMI/
     8.  Computer Resources at GMI(lots of help)/
     9.  GMI Campus Organizations and People/
     10. GMI Falcon Library Catalog <TEL>
     11. General Interest - Non-GMI/
     12. Scholarly and Academic Resources/
     13. Virtual Visitors' Center/
     14. Select this if using a WWW browser and you opened gopher:..du/
<HTML>

Press ? for Help, q to Quit
```

You'll notice that the last line on the screen shows you how to get `Help` and how to `Quit`. Gopher is very user-friendly in that you will always be presented with options on the screen.

The other item of importance is the → in front of option 1. This is my pointer and I can move it by pressing the up and down arrows. If I want to enter some menu option, I can press the right arrow to go into it, or the left arrow to move out of it.

Any menu option which has a slash (/) after it indicates that there are submenu choices under it. Let's choose option 11 (I can just type in the 11 rather than pressing the down arrow).

```
General Interest - Non-GMI

 -->  1.  Auroral Activity
      2.  Computer Software Archives/
      3.  Current Events/
      4.  Education/
      5.  Entertainment/
      6.  Flint Computer Resources - GFEC Hypertext Page <HTML>
      7.  Flint Local Weather Forecast
      8.  General Weather Forecast/
      9.  Libraries/
      10. Miscellaneous Network Services/
      11. Newspapers and Newsmagazines/
      12. Online Books and Journals/
      13. Other gophers/
      14. Politics/
```

I am now given another set of choices. Let's look at choice 12, *Online Books and Journals,* which, again, has submenu choices.

```
Online Books and Journals
 -->  1. Voice of America and Worldnet Television/
      2. A Collection of College Campus Newspapers <HTML>
      3. ACADEME THIS WEEK (Chronicle of Higher Education)/
      4. Annals of Improbable Research(also J.of Irreproducible Results)/
      5. Classics Collections (wiretap.spies.com)/
      6. Computer-Mediated Communication Magazine <HTML>
      7. EDUCOM Documents and News/
      8. Electric Mystics Guide/
      9. Electronic Journals/
      10.Electronic Publications and Resources/
      11.GTOnline from the Colorado City Gazette Telegraph <HTML>
      12.Journals at University of Michigan Library/
      13.Learned NewsWire 1.5 <HTML>
      14.On-Line College Papers (LA Tech Gopher)/
      15.Project Gutenberg/
      16.The Interpedia Project/
      17.Time-Warner Publications Online <HTML>
      18.WIRED Magazine/
```

From here I could enter a host of other choices such as 15, *Project Gutenberg,* which is responsible for taking literature and converting it into an on-line electronic version. Items from the CIA World Factbook to the King James Version of the Bible can be found there.

There are a few public Gopher clients that you can access via Telnet. I have provided a list of the public clients in the U.S. by state:

STATE	HOSTNAME	LOG IN AS
CA	*gopher.ora.com*	gopher
CA	*infopath.ucsd.edu*	infopath
CA	*infoslug.ucsc.edu*	infoslug
CA	*scilibx.ucsc.edu*	gopher
GA	*grits.valdosta.peachnet.edu*	gopher
IL	*gopher.uiuc.edu*	gopher
IL	*ux1.cso.uiuc.edu*	gopher
IA	*panda.uiowa.edu*	panda
MD	*inform.umd.edu*	gopher
MD	*seymour.md.gov*	gopher
MI	*gopher.msu.edu*	gopher
MN	*consultant.micro.umn.edu*	gopher
NC	*gopher.unc.edu*	gopher
NC	*sunsite.unc.edu*	gopher
NC	*twosocks.ces.ncsu.edu*	gopher
OH	*gopher.ohiolink.edu*	gopher
VA	*ecosys.drdr.virginia.edu*	gopher
VA	*gopher.virginia.edu*	gwis
WI	*wsuaix.csc.wsu.edu*	wsuinfo
WI	*telnet.wiscinfo.wisc.edu*	wiscinfo

As previously mentioned, moving around in the original text-based version of Gopher is easy: you use the four *arrow keys*; *space* to go to the next page; and *b* to go back a page. If you have any need for help just push the *?* key. To stop, press *q* and you will be asked if you want to quit *y*(es) or *n*(o). If you want to quit without being asked, press *Q*.

Gopher Server Sites to Start with

Once you have your Gopher client software loaded and configured, point it at these server sites to get started:

ashpool.micro.umn.edu	Washington University archive, Internet Resource Guide
boombox.micro.umn.edu	Gopher distribution archive
chaos.taylored.com	Cypherpunks gopher site
dartcms1.dartmouth.edu	Federal Job openings
deming.eng.clemson.edu	TQM
english-server.hss.cmu.edu	Wide range of subject matter
eryx.syr.edu	Electronic Government Information Service
garnet.msen.com	Internet Business pages
gopher.bu.edu	Boston metropolitan guide

gopher.concert.net	U of NC archives
gopher.cpsr.com	Computer Professionals for Social Responsibility
gopher.eff.org	EFF archive
gopher.house.gov	U.S. House gopher
gopher.msen.com	Search for individuals on the Internet
gopher.uis.itd.umich.edu	U of M archive
hunter.cs.unr.edu	Search Gopherspace using Veronica
infopath.ucsd.edu	Business statistics
internic.net	Internet directory services (lists of lists & sites)
jupiter.sun.csd.unb.ca	FAQs from UseNet
marvel.loc.gov	Library of Congress
metaverse.com	Adam Curry's site
obi.std.com	Phone books, BBS listings, etc.
riceinfo.rice.edu	Business and economics repository
una.hh.lib.umich.edu	Economic bulletin board
wiretap.spies.com	Cyberspace, Humor, etc.
wiretap.spies.com	White House press releases
wx.atmos.uiuc.edu	Weather maps

In addition, these U.S. Gopher sites provide some UseNet News access:

SITE	MENU PATH
aurora.latech.edu	/USENET News
gopher.msu.edu	/News & Weather/USENET news
info-server.lanl.gov	/Network News (USENET)
saturn.wwc.edu	/USENET News via gopher

5.2 USING VERONICA TO SEARCH GOPHERSPACE

Veronica is a Gopher-based resource that you can use to search Gopherspace for menu items that contain words you provide. To start Veronica, you should look for options that say something to the extent of "Search titles in Gopherspace using Veronica." This will often be located under a menu item that says "Other Gopher and Information Services."

You will then typically be presented a menu from which you choose where to run Veronica, and after selecting one of the provided servers, a dialog box will appear asking you what to search for. Veronica is case insensitive when it comes to searching.

Let's take the example that we want to find pictures of trees. Our first attempt might be to say `trees`. Unfortunately we will find too much information on trees, some of it text-based, so we need to narrow our search down using the verbs `and` and `or`. So let's try `trees and pictures`. That probably gives us a little smaller list. We might want to try `trees and (pictures or images)`.

You probably get the idea. The other verbs we could include in our search would be `not`; such as `trees and pictures not wanted` to screen out other people who have requested the same thing we just have. We can also include a * to indicate extra characters at the end of a word such as `trees and pictures not want*` to avoid finding items with want, wanted, and wanting.

Additionally, you can include a `-t flag` option in the search box to tell Veronica to find only certain document types:

LISTING OF VERONICA DOCUMENT TYPES:

0 - Text File	s - Sound
1 - Directory	e - Event
2 - CSO name server	I - Image other than GIF
4 - Mac HQX file	M - MIME message
5 - PC binary	i - Inline text type
6 - UNIX uuencoded file	T - TN3270 session
7 - Full Text Index (Gopher Menu)	c - Calendar
8 - Telnet session	g - Gif image
9 - Binary file	h - HTML

An example of this would be `trees -t g` where we are telling Veronica to only search for gif images of trees.

An Example of Using Veronica

Let's assume that we want to find an online version of the Periodic Table. Gopher would probably be an ideal choice, but I don't know where a Periodic Table is located. I begin by accessing my Gopher software and then point at a Veronica search site:

```
Internet Gopher Information Client v2.0.16

                    Other Gopher and Information Servers

      1.  All the Gopher Servers in the World/
      2.  Search All the Gopher Servers in the World <?>
-->   3.  Search titles in Gopherspace using veronica/
      4.  Africa/
      5.  Asia/
      6.  Europe/
      7.  International Organizations/
      8.  Middle East/
      9.  North America/
      10. Pacific/
      11. Russia/
      12. South America/
      13. Terminal Based Information/
      14. WAIS Based Information/
      15. Gopher Server Registration <??>



Press ? for Help, q to Quit, u to go up a menu                Page: 1/1
```

I notice that option 3 is, *Search titles in gopherspace with Veronica.* This sounds like what I am looking for. I then press *3* or *return* to go to the next menu screen.

```
Internet Gopher Information Client v2.0.16

                    Search titles in Gopherspace using veronica


      3.  Find GOPHER DIRECTORIES by Title word(s) (via NYSERNet) <?>
      4.  Find GOPHER DIRECTORIES by Title word(s) (via PSINet) <?>
      5.  Find GOPHER DIRECTORIES by Title word(s) (via U. Nac. Autonoma .. <?>
      6.  Frequently-Asked Questions (FAQ) about veronica - January 13, 1995
      7.  How to Compose veronica Queries - June 23, 1994
      8.  More veronica: Software, Index-Control Protocol, HTML Pages/
  --> 9.  Search GopherSpace by Title word(s) (via NYSERNet) <?>
      10. Search GopherSpace by Title word(s) (via PSINet) <?>
      11. Search GopherSpace by Title word(s) (via U. Nac. Autonoma de MX.. <?>
          Simplified veronica chooses server - pick a search type:
      13. Simplified veronica: Find Gopher MENUS only <?>
      14. Simplified veronica: find ALL gopher types <?>
      15. how-to-query-veronica
      16. veronica-faq


Press ? for Help, q to Quit, u to go up a menu                  Page: 1/1
```

You can see that I have lots of choices. I am going to select number 9 to perform a search of Gopherspace by a title word. I then see a search screen pop up which prompts me for the words to search for. I will enter Periodic Table at this point.

```
Internet Gopher Information Client v2.0.16

                    Search titles in Gopherspace using veronica


      3.  Find GOPHER DIRECTORIES by Title word(s) (via NYSERNet) <?>
      4.  Find GOPHER DIRECTORIES by Title word(s) (via PSINet) <?>
+------------Search GopherSpace by Title word(s) (via NYSERNet)-------------+
|                                                                           |
| Words to search for                                                       |
|                                                                           |
| periodic table                                                            |
|                                                                           |
| [Help: ^-]  [Cancel: ^G]                                                  |
+---------------------------------------------------------------------------+
      13. Simplified veronica: Find Gopher MENUS only <?>
```

```
     14. Simplified veronica: find ALL gopher types <?>
     15. how-to-query-veronica
     16. veronica-faq


Press ? for Help, q to Quit, u to go up a menu                  Page: 1/1
```

After a few seconds, the following list of periodic tables is shown. I could then type in the number of the option to view, or move the arrow keys to point to my choice and press *return*.

```
Internet Gopher Information Client v2.0.16

     Search GopherSpace by Title word(s) (via NYSERNet): periodic table

 --> 1.  Periodic Table of Elements/
     2.  Periodic Table of the Elements
     3.  Periodic Table
     4.  Periodic Table
     5.  Periodic Table, Facts & Copyright
     6.  Periodic Table
     7.  Periodic Table
     8.  Periodic Table
     9.  Re: Periodic Table of the Elements
     10. Periodic Table of the Elements
     11. Re: Periodic Table of the Elements
     12. Periodic Table
     13. xpt              [volume19]:  xpt          - An X Periodic Table/
     14. xpt              [volume20]:  xpt          - An X Periodic Table/
     15. [volume19] xpt            :  xpt           - An X Periodic Table/
     16. [volume20] xpt            :  xpt           - An X Periodic Table/
     17. xview_periodic    : XVIEW Periodic table   - Illustrates objects i../
     18. Periodic_Table.ps

Press ? for Help, q to Quit, u to go up a menu                  Page: 1/12
```

5.3 USING JUGHEAD TO SEARCH GOPHERSPACE

Jughead is a tool very similar to Veronica with one major difference: Veronica tries to look at all of Gopherspace in general; Jughead looks at a confined space in depth. Jughead is not nearly as widespread as Veronica since Jughead requires the systems administrator at each Gopher site to construct a local database for Jughead to use. When Jughead's search window pops up, you can fill it out exactly as you did for Veronica.

If you want to try a Jughead search, point your Gopher client to the University of Utah's Gopher site *gopher.utah.edu*. In addition, you can get a list of all Jughead servers from this site by selecting the *all known Jughead servers* menu option.

In addition to the standard boolean searches that we performed on Veronica, Jughead supports a few special ones:

`?all` *`what`*	Returns all matches on search string what
`?help [command]`	Returns help document and any optional matches for the command given
`?limit=`*`n what`*	Returns up to n items matching the search string *what*

5.4 A FINAL GOPHER USE

The Gopher at the University of Wisconsin at Madison has a main menu option labeled *Phone Books* which contains white pages of folks on the Internet. Another Gopher site with this type of data is the Gopher at Notre Dame *gopher.nd.edu* which has a menu option *Non-Notre Dame Information Sources/Phone Books-Other Institutions*. From this point you have access to hundreds of white page directories for schools, companies and the government.

Another good source for college e-mail addresses can be FTP-ed from *pit-manager.mit.edu* in the directory */pub/usenet/soc.college*.

5.5 WAIS

WAIS (pronounced "ways") is a Wide Area Information Server that searches for words in documents. WAIS goes beyond Gopher, FTP and Archie in that it searches for all kinds of information: text, sounds, programs, graphic images and animation.

How Do I Use WAIS?

There are two ways to use WAIS:

1) use a local WAIS program on your computer
2) Telnet to a public WAIS client or through e-mail.

Both methods work fundamentally the same way; a box will pop up and request keywords to search for. The following is a listing of Public U.S. WAIS Clients by state:

STATE	HOSTNAME	LOG IN AS:
CA	*swais.cwis.uci.edu*	swais
MA	*nnsc.nsf.net*	wais
MA	*quake.think.com*	wais
NC	*kudzu.cnidr.org*	wais
NC	*sunsite.unc.edu*	swais

An Example of Using WAIS

Let's start by Telneting to *sunsite.unc.edu*. Once we log in as *swais*, we should type `vt100` when prompted for the terminal type.

```
nova{sjames}20% telnet sunsite.unc.edu
Trying 152.2.254.81 ...
Connected to sunsite.unc.edu.
Escape character is '^]'.
```

```
UNIX(r) System V Release 4.0 (calzone)

***************** Welcome to SunSITE.unc.edu *****************

SunSITE offers several public services via login. These include:

Lynx is broken temporarily. It'll be back shortly.

Use lynx the simple WWW client to access gopher and Web areas
For a simple WAIS client (over 500 databases),  login as swais
For WAIS search of political databases,         login as politics
For WAIS search of LINUX databases,             login as linux

For a FTP session, ftp to sunsite.unc.edu. Then login as anonymous

For more information about SunSITE, send mail to info@sunsite.unc.edu

login: swais
Last login: Mon Aug 19 11:02:16 from nova.gmi.edu

University of North Carolina Office For Information Technology
in cooperation with Sun Microsystems, Inc.

Materials available via this id are subject to the statements in
DISCLAIMER.readme found in the anonymous ftp area or on the main menu
of the SunSITE.unc.edu gopher

You could be running this code on your own machine.
You'll find it and other WAIS stuff available via anonymous ftp
from SunSITE.unc.edu in the pub/packages/infosystems/wais directory.

These databases are also available via gopher.
Just point your gopher client to sunsite.unc.edu 70
and enjoy using these databases from your gopher interface.

you're probably a vt100 or should be
TERM = (unknown) vt100
```

We are now presented with a screen listing the various databases. We need to select our sources, which we do by using the *arrow keys*. We press the *space bar* to select a source and an asterisk appears to indicate that we have selected the source. Don't worry about the cost field, all the sources are free! You can select as many sources as you wish before searching. If you are going to start a new search, you should press the = key to clear out all your old sources if you don't intend to search all of them.

```
SWAIS                         Source Selection                  Sources: 82
  #            Server                      Source                      Cost
001:    [     sunsite.unc.edu]  alt-sys-sun                            Free
002:    [                    ]  American-Music-Resource                Free
003:    [                    ]  avi_files                              Free
```

```
004:    [              calypso]  bush-speeches                          Free
005:    [                     ]  carter-oh                              Free
006:    [                     ]  clinton-speeches                       Free
007:    [                     ]  clinton-speeches                       Free
008:    [      sunsite.unc.edu]  Community-IdeaNet                      Free
009:    [                     ]  Davis-eis-cds                          Free
010:    [                     ]  Davis-eiscds                           Free
011:    [                     ]  Davis-music-eam                        Free
012:    [                     ]  Davis-music-jazz                       Free
013:    [                     ]  Davis-music-rbr                        Free
014:    [                     ]  Davis-music-vids                       Free
015:    [calypso-2.oit.unc.ed]  Dr-Fun                                  Free
016:    [                     ]  eisenhower-oh                          Free
017:    [      sunSITE.unc.edu]  eric-digests                           Free
018:    [      sunsite.unc.edu]  Fascism                                Free

Keywords:

<space> selects, w for keywords, arrows move, <return> searches, q quits, or ?
```

Once you have selected your sources, press *return* to go to the keywords line. Enter all the keywords you want to match. Let's say that we want to search for President Clinton's health care reforms. I might enter `Clinton health reform`. After you've entered your keywords press *return* to start the search.

```
SWAIS                        Source Selection                  Sources: 82
 #           Server                       Source                Cost
019:    [           bittyblue]  foo                                    Free
020:    [                    ]  ford-finding-aids                      Free
021:    [calypso-2.oit.unc.ed]  freeburma                              Free
022:    [             calypso]  govnii                                 Free
023:    [             calypso]  govnpr                                 Free
024:  * [             calypso]  govradio                               Free
025:  * [ calypso.oit.unc.edu]  Health-Security-Act                    Free
026:  * [           president]  index                                  Free
027:    [             calypso]  INFO                                   Free
028:    [     sunsite.unc.edu]  Jainist-texts                          Free
029      calypso-2.oit.unc.ed]  java                                   Free
030:    [                    ]  johnson-oh                             Free
031:    [             calypso]  lawrence-obrien-interview              Free
032:    [     sunsite.unc.edu]  linux-addresses                        Free
033                          ]  linux-faq                              Free
034:    [             calypso]  linux-gcc-faq                          Free
035:    [             calypso]  linux-net-faq                          Free
036:    [                    ]  linux-software-map                     Free

Keywords: Clinton health reform
```

Once the search is done, you can perform another search or you can examine what was returned by simply moving to the appropriate line and pressing *return*.

WAIS will then contact the source of the document and pull up a copy of the document. If you like what you see and want to keep a copy of it, press either *s* for save or *m* for mail. As usual, you can use *q* to stop viewing a document. Be careful though, because *q* also quits the WAIS program.

5.6 PERFORMING A WAIS SEARCH VIA E-MAIL

Performing a WAIS search over e-mail is fairly simple. Send a message to *wais-mail@quake.think.com* with a message body of *search sourcename keywords. Sourcename* is the database name(s) to search and *keywords* are what you want to search for. When you get your results back, you can retrieve the documents by sending another e-mail message to the server with a message body of *retrieve DocID*. The *DocID* will be supplied along with your WAIS results.

5.7 THE FUTURE OF WAIS

As you may have noticed, this WAIS section was very short. The reason for this is that the future of WAIS may be limited. There are several publicly available search engines on the World Wide Web that do as good a job as WAIS without having to specify any databases. We will spend time examining this type of search later. As search systems become more integrated into packages, WAIS may indeed become an archaic system.

CHAPTER SUMMARY

This chapter examined the Internet entities Gopher and WAIS. Both of these resources provide a menu-based approach to retrieving information from the Internet. The primary difference between the two resources lies in the fact that WAIS requires that the user select databases from which a search is executed, while Gopher simply allows the entry of keywords, and then gopherspace is examined for matching information. The future of both of these items is in doubt due to the exponential growth of web browsers and the publicly available search engines which can be accessed by them.

KEY TERMS

Client
Document
Gopher
Gopherspace
Item
Jughead
Server
Veronica
WAIS

PROBLEMS

1. Find out if your school has a Gopher site. Use your Gopher software to access it.
2. Point your Gopher client at *gopher.house.gov* and find out who your state representatives are. Print out the information on one of your representatives. (Note: if you don't have a Gopher client, Telnet to one of the publicly available ones.)
3. Use Veronica to find out where the Periodic Tables are stored on the web. Then locate and print out the information related to the element molybdenum.
4. Use WAIS to look up what President Bush had to say about reform. Try using "bush-speeches" as your data source and "reform" as your keyword.

CHAPTER

6

The World Wide Web & HTML

SCIENCE/ENGINEERING SPOTLIGHT: ROBOTICS

We often think of robots as being mobile machines matched with artificial intelligence. Science fiction books and movies have definitely contributed their share to this viewpoint: R2-D2 and C-3PO from *Star Wars* come to mind. Today, robots really are best suited for helping with the manufacturing process. Robots can help in assembly and inspection operations and in packaging/palette loading. In addition, many robots today have special end effectors which allow them to perform welding, material removal, painting and adhesive application.

OBJECTIVES

This chapter will examine what is considered the state of the art with respect to the Internet today: the World Wide Web. Web browsers and their capabilities are examined. The chapter then provides information on creating HTML Web pages. The chapter concludes with a look at some of the newer extensions to the Web in the form of JAVA (a scripting language) and VRML (which allows 3D movement on Web pages). Let's start by looking at what WWW is all about.

6.1 WWW - THE WORLD WIDE WEB

All the other services that we have viewed up to this point have been primarily text in nature. The Web, although it has a text side, was primarily designed to be graphical in nature. In fact, web browsers are a point and click approach to accessing the Internet.

WWW has combined text, graphics, audio and even animation into a multimedia event. Each page that you view with your web browser is typically linked to other pages around the Internet, and you can directly hop from location to location with the click of a mouse. Should a particular page have an audio file, your computer can retrieve and play that sound if your computer is equipped with audio capabilities. You don't have to just look at plain graphic screens; your computer can download moving images and play them for you.

The best feature of the Web is probably the fact that the same interface is used to move around the Internet and to seamlessly access Internet services such as FTP, Gopher and UseNet News while supplying powerful search engines that are starting to replace WAIS.

WWW-Related Terms

The following is a list of terms that deal with the World Wide Web. You should familiarize yourself with these terms before moving on.

Browsers: A browser is simply the program that you use to access the hypertext documents on the web. Browsers are also responsible for showing you animations, graphics and playing sounds if your computer has such capability. Browsers come in two flavors: text and graphics.

Text browsers show you only the text on each of the pages; however, you can jump between pages by pressing the cursor keys. There are two main text browsers available: *WWW* and *Lynx*.

Graphic browsers are the full blown programs that you usually see when someone says they're "surfing the 'Net." There are several graphic browsers used today: *Mosaic*™, Microsoft's *Internet Explorer*™ and *Netscape Navigator*™.

Within any browser you have the ability to configure other programs that can handle a specific document type. For example, if I wanted to, I could set my PC up to run a sound player when the browser encounters any .au file. In this respect, you can upgrade your computer to take advantage of whatever aspects of the Web you feel are important.

HTTP: Hypertext Transport Protocol is the protocol which allows the hypertext pages on the Web to be quickly retrieved.

Home Pages: Most WWW users can create their own home page which may have information on the user, or may serve as a repository for the user's favorite Web sites. Home pages, as well as any other Web page, must be built with HTML. There are many programs available that can help a user quickly create HTML pages. The second half of this chapter will assist you in creating HTML pages.

HTML: HTML is the special formatting that is used to create one of the pages on the Web. HTML stands for Hypertext Markup Language and is a set of basic commands that are placed around objects in a document that tell how an object is to be displayed, where the object is to be located, how to link to another page, and so on.

Hypertext: This is simply text that contains a link to some other object. You will know when a particular text is hypertext since it will be a different color than normal text (on some browsers it may be underlined). Documents that contain more than just text that forms links are called *hypermedia.*

Links: Links are references to other documents on the Web.

URL: URL stands for Uniform Resource Locator which is a Web standard on how to locate an item that is to be retrieved. There are two types of URLs: *absolute,* which requires the full computer name, path name and item name, and *relative,* which assumes that the previous computer and directory names are to be used. A typical URL might look like *http://defiant.gmi.edu/~sjames.*

As you might have guessed, the first part of the URL is the *protocol service* to use. After the colon and the two slashes come the *computer name* and *path name.* The very end of the URL contains the *item name.* Our example then tells the browser to retrieve the item *sjames* from the computer *defiant.gmi.edu* using the *http* protocol.

Other protocols that can be used in a browser include:

SERVICE	USE
archie	starts an Archie session
finger	starts up the finger program
ftp	starts an FTP session
gopher	starts a Gopher session
mailto	starts an e-mailer program
news	starts a UseNet News session
telnet	starts a TELNET session
wais	accesses a WAIS server
whois	accesses a whois server

Web Server: A web server is a computer which contains home pages that are to be supplied to browsers that wish to view them.

A Sample Web Browser

Notice how much more meaning can be conveyed from information retrieved from a graphical web browser when compared to plain text:

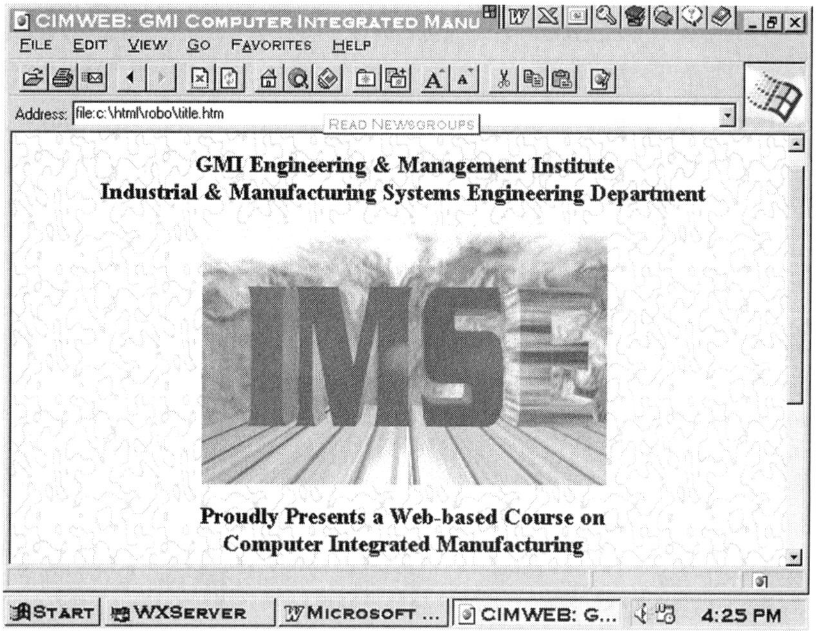

Finding Out More About WWW

If you want to find out more about the Web and what can be done with it, here are a few places to start:

USENET NEWSGROUPS

comp.infosystems.www.misc	- how to do anything else
comp.infosystems.www.providers	- how to set up a WWW server
comp.infosystems.www.users	- how to use and set up client software

MAILING LISTS

You can send e-mail to *listserv@info.cern.ch* with the body message of *subscribe <list> yourrealname.*

The list needs to be one of the following:

www-announce	- discusses current state and new software
www-html	- talks about the html language
www-talk	- technical discussions of WWW software design

WWW SITES	
http://info.cern.ch/hypertext/WWW/TheProject.html	World Wide Web Initiative
http://www.ncsa.uiuc.edu/demoweb/demo.html	NCSA Mosaic Demo Document
http://www.internic.net	InterNIC
http://www.eit.com/web/www.guide	Entering the WWW: A Guide to Cyberspace

A Few Web Sites to Start with

If you're new on the Web and want a few neat sites to play around with, you might want to check these out:

http://defiant.gmi.edu	The coolest professors hang out here
http://galaxy.einet.net/galaxy.html	EINet Galaxy Search Engine
http://hypatia.gsfc.nasa.gov/NASA_homepage.html	NASA
http://info.er.usgs.gov	U.S. Geological Survey
http://lcweb.loc.gov/homepage/lchp.html	Library of Congress
http://med-www.Stanford.EDU/MedCenter/welcome.html	Stanford Univ. Med. Center
http://metaverse.com	Adam Curry's site
http://mistral.enst.fr/louvre	The Louvre online
http://netvet.wustl.edu/e-zoo.htm	Electronic Zoo
http://pubweb.parc.xerox.com/map	Xerox PARC Map Viewer
http://shop.internic.net	Internet Shopping Network
http://tns-www.lcs.mit.edu/tns-www.home.html	MIT Cutting Edge
http://voyager.paramount.com	*Star Trek: Voyager* site
http://wings.buffalo.edu/world/	Virtual Tourist
http://www.cl.cam.ac.uk/coffee/coffee.html	The Trojan Room Coffee Machine
http://www.commerce.net	CommerceNet
http://www.fedworld.gov	FedWorld
http://www.hotwired.com	*HotWired* Magazine
http://www.internet.nic/directories.html	Infoworld's web page
http://www.internic.net	InterNIC Home Page
http://www.microsoft.com	Microsoft web page
http://www.msstate.edu/Movies	Cardiff's Movie Database
http://www.os.dhhs.gov	U.S. Dept. of Health & Human Serv.
http://www.scotborders.co.uk:80/dryburgh/dryburghmap.html	An area map
http://www.timeinc.com/pathfinder/Welcome.html	Time/Warner's Pathfinder
http://www.whitehouse.gov	The White House
http://www.worldbank.org	The World Bank

Search Sites

Where can you go if you are looking for something on the Web, but don't know where it is located or what it is called? You need to use a search engine. The following is a list of the more popular sites:

Alta Vista	*http://www.altavista.com*
ArchiePlex	*http://pubweb.nexor.co.uk/public/archie/archieplex doc/form.html*
EINET	*http://www.einet.net/www/www.html*
Excite	*http://www.excite.com*
Lycos	*http://lycos.cs.cmu.edu*
Spry Internet Wizard	*http://www.spry.com/wizard/index.html*
WebCrawler	*http://webcrawler.cs.washington.edu/WebCrawler/ WebQuery.html*
Whole Internet Catalog	*http://www.gnn.com/wic/newrescat.toc.html*
World Wide Web Word	*http://www.cs.colorado.edu/home/mcbryan/www.html*
Yahoo	*http://www.yahoo.com*

PRACTICE!

This practice set is concerned with using a web browser.

1) Try using your browser to view the home page of my department, which is located at the URL: *http://defiant.gmi.edu.* If you are successful you should see a page similar to the one shown above in the sample web browser example.
2) Point your web browser to URL *http://www.yahoo.com.* Try entering *Clinton health reform* in the search box. Notice how much easier this searching is in comparison to using Veronica or WAIS.

6.2 CREATING WEB PAGES WITH HTML

HTML pages can be created in several different ways. There are graphical Web creation tools that provide users with tool palettes from which the different HTML elements may be selected. HTML pages can also be created with just a simple text editor.

While the text editor may be a little more time consuming to work with, it is important to note that all HTML pages are actually text-based. This section will provide an introduction to creating HTML pages from a completely text-based view.

Once you have created an HTML page, you must put the page on a Web server so that other users on the Internet can see your page. It is beyond the scope of this module to explain to you where to put the page, how to get the page on the Web server and so forth. Even the name of the initial HTML page may have to be something specific such as Welcome.html or Home.html. Therefore, it is important that you obtain some help in answering these issues which are specific to your computer resources.

You should bear in mind that none of these factors will limit you in creating HTML pages. You can still create a page on whatever computer has a browser. After the page is created, simply point the browser at the page to view it.

The Basic HTML Page

All HTML pages have the following skeleton form:

```
<HTML>
<BODY>
</BODY>
</HTML>
```

HTML uses what are known as "tags." You put tags around items that are to appear in your HTML page. The tag acts as a display attribute for a given item. For example, if I wanted to underline some text on an HTML page, I would need to turn on the underlining feature, type the text that I want underlined, and then turn off the underlining feature. This turning on and turning off process is simply the use of a tag.

From the given skeleton form, you can see that all HTML pages must start with the <HTML> tag. Anything that appears inside of the < > marks is part of the HTML language and will not literally be shown on the HTML page. Just as all pages start with <HTML>, they must end with </HTML>. Most tags use a / character to indicate that some attribute is to be turned off.

The <BODY> and </BODY> tags are where we will place the meat of our HTML work.

Let's now put together a little more complex example, in which I am going to add some information to be displayed on my HTML page.

```
<HTML>
<! *************************************************>
<! *                Example.html                   *>
<! *************************************************>
<! *           Created by: Scott D. James          *>
<! *                   On: June 11, 1996           *>
<! *************************************************>
<! * Purpose: To show a simple HTML page.           *>
<! *************************************************>
<TITLE>Scott's First Page</TITLE>
<BODY>
<H1>Hello to the Internet from Scott!</H1>
<P>
I'm glad you stopped by...
<BR>
Created 06/11/96 by Scott D. James
</BODY>
</HTML>
```

Notice that both the <HTML> and <BODY> tags appear in addition to a host of new tags. The first new tag starts with <! . This tag indicates that I want to put some comments into the HTML source. These comments will not be shown on the HTML page, but might be nice to document how or why I did something. Anything between the <! > is the comment.

The next tag is the <TITLE> tag. This indicates that what follows this tag will appear in the title of the browser's window. If you examine the actual browser screen below, you will notice the title says "Scott's First Page." An accompanying </TITLE> must be used to end the title bar text.

Following the <TITLE> section is the <BODY> section, which again usually contains the main information that is to be displayed on the HTML page. I surrounded some text with the <H1> and </H1> tags. These are used to indicate that I wanted the text to be displayed with a bold heading type of appearance.

The <P> tag is simply a paragraph marker, which inserts the blank line between the header and the regular text. You need to realize that return keystrokes placed in the HTML source file are for our purposes only; HTML ignores those returns and will only process the HTML tags that are placed in the source.

The next line is some text that I simply want printed out. I used the <BR> tag to separate the two lines on the HTML page. Think BR, as in line break, which is how we get returns to show up on our pages.

Finally, I use the </BODY> and </HTML> tags to end the body section and HTML section. Here's how the page appears in a browser:

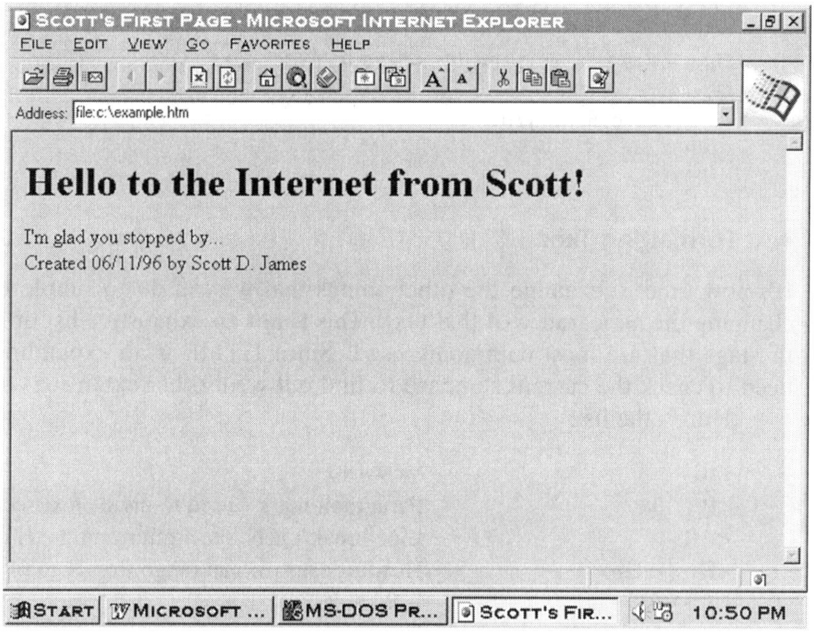

The HTML page has a pretty nice appearance for the little bit of work that it took to create it. You should also realize by now that tags surround text and act as attributes of how that text is to be displayed. You should see that tags can be placed inside of other tags and that HTML can be written as a long line if we so desire. For example,

```
<HTML><TITLE>Hi There!</TITLE><BODY>Isn't this fun?</BODY></HTML>
```

is perfectly valid.

You should try creating a simple HTML page and viewing it with a browser before moving on. Any text editor such as MS-DOS's *edit* or UNIX's *vi* will work fine. Probably the biggest mistake that you will encounter is forgetting to close “ ” or < >. If you don't close these items, the browser you are using will do its best to try to display the HTML page. If things don't look the way they should, check to ensure items have been properly closed.

Practice!

Let's create an HTML page that has the following information on it: the author's name and the slogan “I love HTML!” The slogan should be very large in size. Let's also put the title “HMTL Is Easy” on the title bar.

You should type in the following code, save it and then view it with your browser.

```
<HTML>
<TITLE>HTML Is Easy</TITLE>
<BODY>
This page was written by (* your name here *)<BR>
<P>
<H1>I Love HTML!</H1>
</BODY>
</HTML>
```

Text Formatting Tags

It's now time to examine the other things that we can do to simple text in terms of changing the appearance of that text. This is not an exhaustive list of tags, but rather, the tags that are most commonly used. Since HTML is an expanding universe, you need to check the current standard to find out what other extensions are available.

Here's the list:

TAG	MEANING
<P>	Paragraph mark - used to divide text sections
 	Line break - acts like a return on the HTML page
<Hn> </Hn>	Heading tags - *n* can range from 1 to 6
<B> </B>	Bold text
<I> </I>	Italics text
<U> </U>	Underlined text
<BLOCKQUOTE> </BLOCKQUOTE>	Double indented text
<NOBR> </NOBR>	No line breaks in text

<CENTER> </CENTER>	Center
<CODE> </CODE>	Computer code
<PRE> </PRE>	Keeps tabs and breaks as they appear in the editor (PREformatted)

Let's look at some of these tags through the browser's eye:

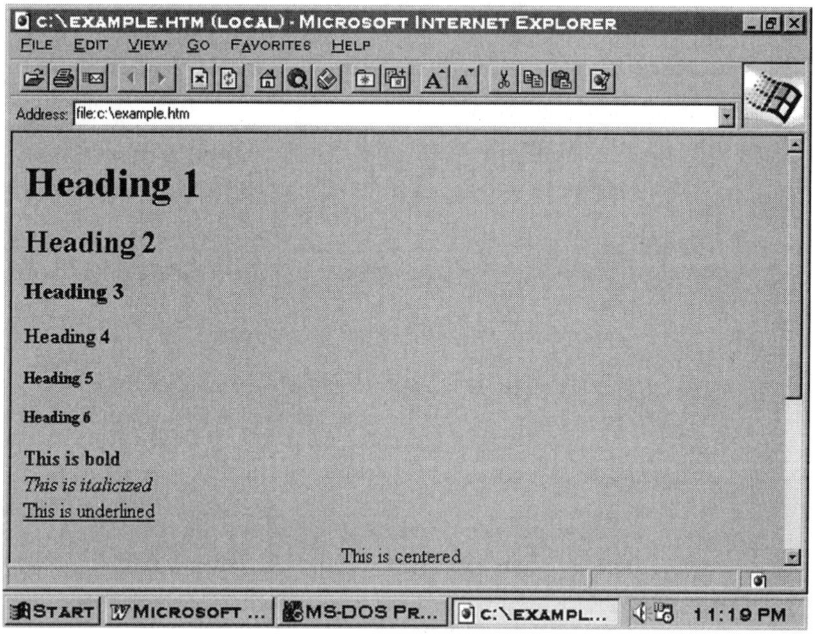

Here's the accompanying HTML code that produced that page:

```
<HTML>
<BODY>
<H1>Heading 1</H1> <H2>Heading 2</H2>
<H3>Heading 3</H3> <H4>Heading 4</H4>
<H5>Heading 5</H5> <H6>Heading 6</H6> <P>
<B>This is bold</B><BR>
<I>This is italicized</I><BR>
<U>This is underlined</U><BR><BR>
<CENTER>This is centered</CENTER>
<P>
```

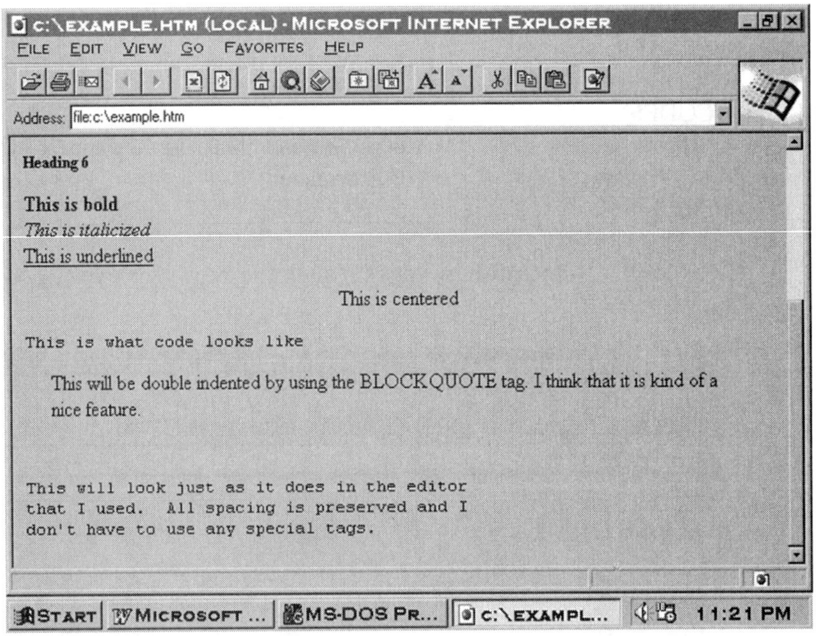


```
<CODE>This is what code looks like<CODE><BR>
<BLOCKQUOTE>This will be double indented by using the BLOCKQUOTE tag. I
think
that it is kind of a nice feature.</BLOCKQUOTE><BR>
<PRE>
This will look just as it does in the editor
that I used.  All spacing is preserved and I
don't have to use any special tags.
</PRE>
</BODY>
</HTML>
```

Other Text Gadgets

One common task that we often need to perform in our HTML pages is that of creating lists. There are two types of lists that we can create: unordered (or bulleted) and ordered (or numbered).

Unordered lists have the skeleton frame of:

```
<UL>
[<UL TYPE = [circle|disk|square]>]
<LI>First choice
<LI>Second choice
```

```
<LI>nth choice
</UL>
```

Unordered lists use the circle as the default list item divider. If you want, you can change the circle to a disk or square by supplying the `UL TYPE` tag.

Ordered lists look very similar except that we use OL instead of UL. The `OL TYPE` can be one of:

a - Lowercase letter numbers
A - Uppercase letter numbers
i - Lowercase roman numbers
I - Uppercase roman numbers
1 - Arabic numbers (this is the default)

Here's how to create a nested list (a list within a list) using several of the list elements:

```
<HTML>
<BODY>
<UL>
<LI>Things I like about HTML:
<OL>
<LI>It's fun
<LI>It's easy
<LI>It's fast
</OL>
<LI>Things I like about the Internet:
<OL>
<OL TYPE=i>
<LI>It's easy to use
<LI>My friends are using it
<LI>Anyone can contact me 24 hours a day
<LI>It's a lot of fun
</OL>
</UL>
</BODY>
</HTML>
```

This page shows up as the following on the browser (*see next page*):

Sometimes it's nice to break up a long page with some lines. The `<HR>` Horizontal Rule tag is perfect for this job. These are its uses:

`<HR>`	
`<HR SIZE=n>`	The line will be *n* points high
`<HR NOSHADE>`	Plain line
`<HR WIDTH=[n|p%]>`	The line will be *n* pixels long or *p*% of the page

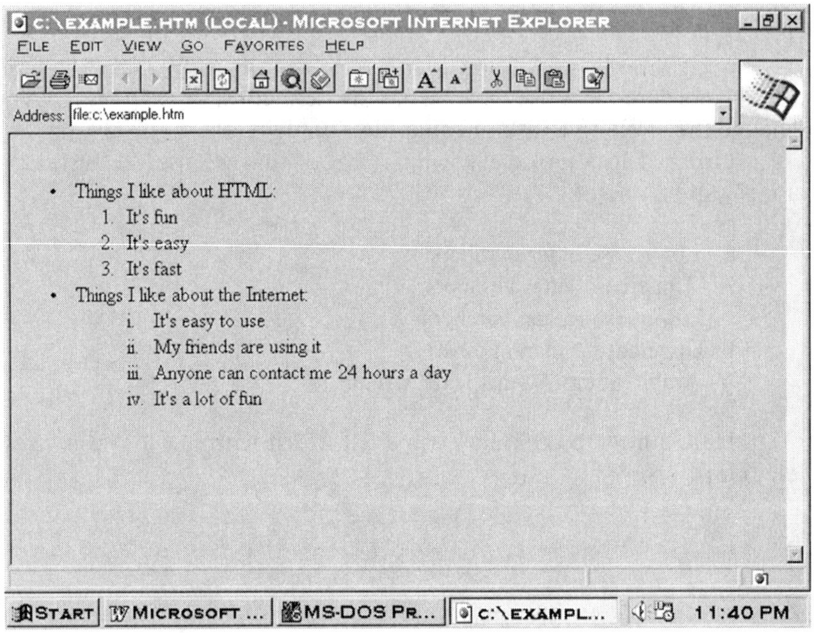

Here's an example of the 4 types in the browser:

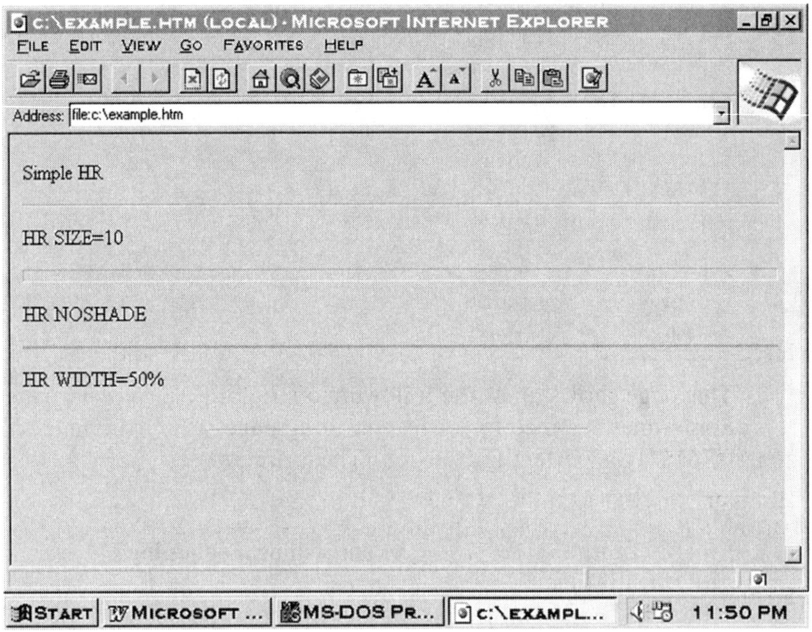

Working with Images

Text is only one feature that can be included in HTML pages. The other item that we frequently see is graphics. If you have any gif formatted images that you wish to display in your HTML page, use the `IMG SRC` tag. The format is:

```
<IMG SRC="URL to image"
[ALIGN="TOP|BOTTOM|MIDDLE|LEFT|RIGHT|TEXTTOP|ABSMIDDLE|BASELINE"]
[ALT="text"] [BORDER=n] [VSPACE=n] [HSPACE=n]>
```

where,

- "URL to image" is the path to the graphics file and the name of the graphics file
- ALIGN refers to the alignment of the image
- ALT refers to text that is to be displayed in place of the image in text-based browsers
- BORDER refers to the point width (*n*) of the border that surrounds the image
- VSPACE offsets the image *n* points from the left/right margin of the page
- HSPACE offsets the image *n* points from the upper/lower margin of the page

Let's take a look at some of this in action with the following HTML page:

```
<HTML>
<BODY>
<! Just stick the image in>
<IMG SRC="\HTML\IMSE.GIF">
<P>
<! Let's put the image in and flow the text around it>
<! Also notice the ALT tag so that text based viewers can see something>
<IMG SRC="\HTML\IMSE.GIF" ALT="IMSE logo image" ALIGN="LEFT" HSPACE=10>
This text should appear<BR>
next to the image on the<BR>
right hand side of the page<BR>
<P>
</BODY>
</HTML>
```

Here's the resulting browser page (*see next page*) (note that the full second image is on the page; I just didn't scroll down far enough to show it):

Creating Links

Links are the last item that we need to examine to have a well-rounded view of HTML. The magic behind the Web is the ability to leap from page to page. This leaping is what is known as a link. Any displayable entity on an HTML page can become a link. The format for a link is:

```
<A HREF="URL to link to">Item-to-show-up-as-the-link</A>
```

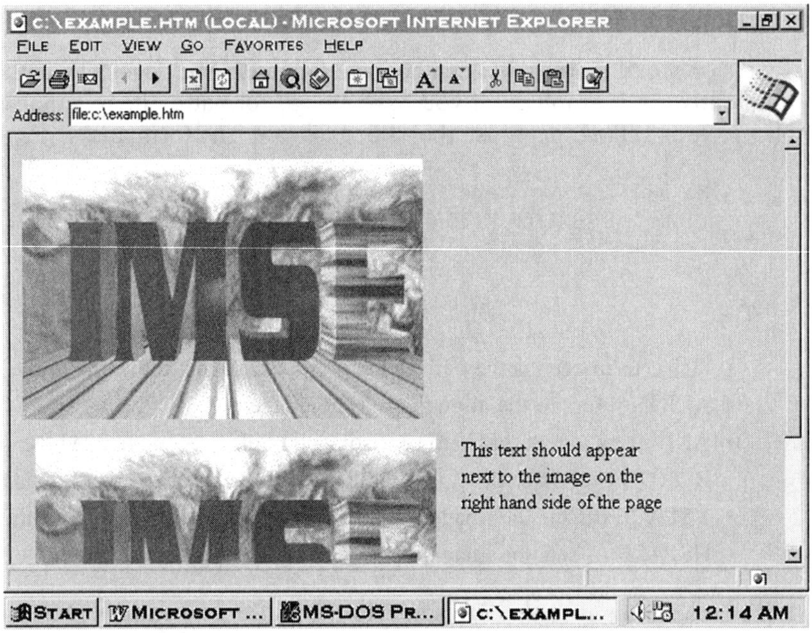

The A comes from Anchor. If you make text a link, it will show up in a different color from other text. If you make an image a link, the border around the image will be a different color. Let's create two pages and make the pages link to each other.

PAGE 1 HTML CODE:

```
<HTML>
<BODY>
<CENTER><H2>Welcome to Page 1!</H2></CENTER>
<A HREF="\page2.htm"><IMG SRC="\HTML\IMSE.GIF" BORDER=7></A>
<CENTER>Click the image or <A HREF="\page2.htm">here</A> to go to Page
2.
</CENTER>
</BODY>
</HTML>
```

PAGE 2 HTML CODE:

```
<HTML>
<BODY>
<H2>Welcome to page 2!</H2>
Here's the way to <A HREF="\page1.htm">Page 1</A>.
</BODY>
</HTML>
```

Here's what Page 1 looks like in the browser:

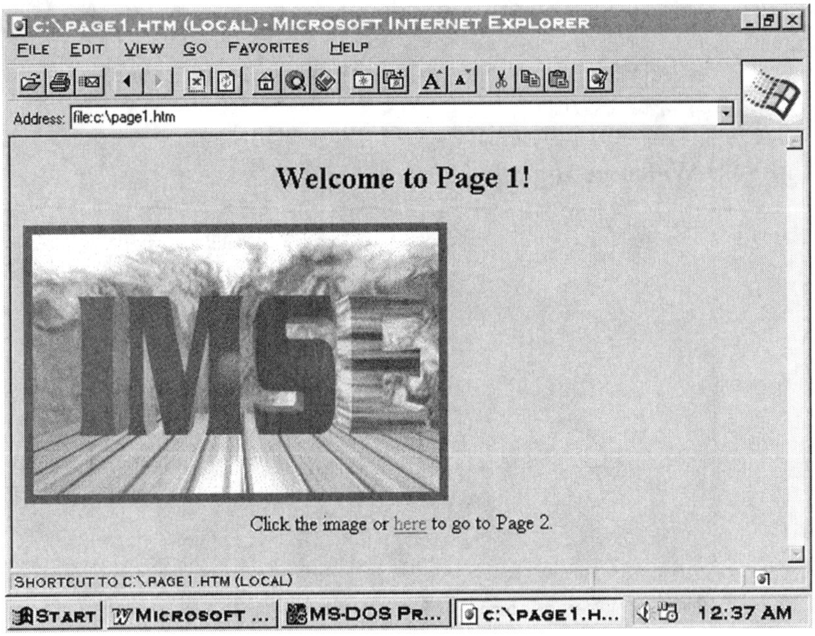

Notice that both the image and the word "here" in the text line are a different color from the rest of the material on the page. Both of those items are links to another HTML page. If I click in either spot, I get to the second page (*see next page*):

As you can see, Page 2 provides a text link to go back to page 1.

Many times the links that we make are not on our own local machine. This doesn't present a problem as long as we identify the remote machine in our URL. For example, I could make a link to a page on my remote machine *defiant*. This is what the link might look like: `<A HREF="http://defiant.gmi.edu">To IMSE Homepage</A>`

By carefully setting a remote computer's name and service that you wish to use, you can significantly enhance HTML pages that you are designing. Here's some other examples:

```
<A HREF="telnet://nova.gmi.edu>Click here to telnet to nova</A>
<A HREF="mailto://sjames@nova.gmi.edu>Mail sjames</A>
<A HREF="ftp://oak.oakland.edu>FTP to Oakland University</A>
```

6.3 VRML

VRML is an extension that has been added to several browsers. VRML stands for Virtual Reality Markup Language. VRML allows HTML pages to be created that allow a user to actually move through and interact with an image on a page. For example, Microsoft provides a VRML page which has their campus on it. Under the campus are

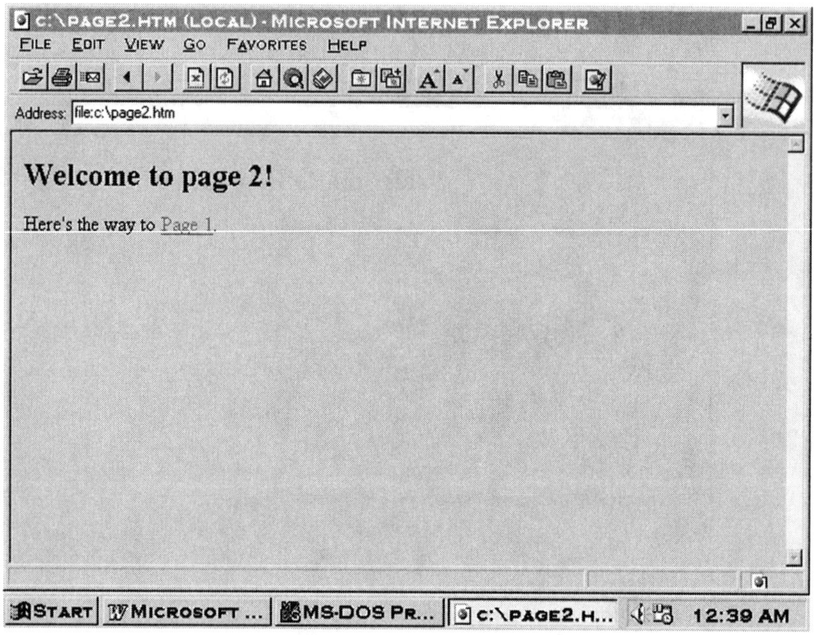

buttons that allow the user to move left, right, up and down. Additionally the user can change the perspective and zoom both in and out of the image.

To use VRML, you must download a VRML add-in for your browser. After you have installed the VRML extension, simply point your browser at a VRML site to try it out. Look at the home page for whichever browser you have for more information on VRML add-in availability. Here's a sample VRML page reprinted with the permission of Silicon Graphics, Inc. (*see next page*):

Here are some VRML sites to try out:

http://webspace.sgi.com/intro.html	Silicon Graphics Inc.'s VRML Page
http://www.cybertown.com	Cybertown
http:://www.paperinc.com/wrls.html	Paper Software Inc.'s Worlds Page
http://www.planet9.com	Planet 9 Studios

6.4 JAVA

Java is the current hot topic related to the World Wide Web and the Internet. Java is a programming language which allows client/server applications to be developed and run on the Internet. Java looks quite similar to the programming language C++ in its design.

Why Java is so important right now is the idea that someday you will run applications right off of the Internet, thus reducing what you need to have loaded locally on your own computer. Some companies see the future as a time in which you simply point your browser at the applet (Javatalk for an application) you need to run,

such as a word processor, and you will lease that application for a few cents each time you use it.

The whole computer industry is abuzz when it comes to Java, but only time will tell where its future lies. There are some Java applets currently available, however, you must have a Java-capable browser in order to use them.

6.5 A LAST RESORT TO THE WEB

If you have a desperate need to try out the Web and don't have any other way to access it, there are a few public web browser sites that can be Telneted to. These sites run an incredibly poor text-based web browser. Nevertheless, at least you will be on the Web. This text-based browser is most likely either Lynx or WWW.

U.S. PUBLIC TEXT WWW BROWSERS BY STATE:

KS	*ukanaix.cc.ukans.edu*	(login as kufacts)
NJ	*www.njit.edu*	(login as www)
NC	*www.unc.edu*	(login as lynx)
NY	*fatty.law.cornell.edu*	(login as www)

Here are the commands you'll need:

TEXT-BASED LYNX AND WWW COMMANDS:

Command	Full name	Description
-	number	Follow the specified link
b	back	Jump to previous document in recall list

bo	bottom	Jump to the end of the current document
f *words*	find *words*	Use specified keywords to search index
g *URL*	go	Jump to specified document or resource
h	help	Display command summary and technical info
ho	home	Jump to the starting document
l	list	Display a list of links within current document
m	manual	Jump to the browser reference document
n	next	Jump to the next link within the last document
p	previous	Jump to the previous link within the last document
-	quit	Quit the web
r	recall	Display list of previously visited documents
r *number*	recall *number*	Jump to specified document from the recall list
-	RETURN	Display next screenful of information
t	top	Jump to the beginning of the current document
u	up	Display previous screenful of current document

I really would try to stay away from using this. Getting your own web browser working is worth the effort that it takes! Text-based public WWW sites are an extremely poor example of what the Web has to offer.

Here's an example of the IMSE Department's home page viewed from Lynx:

```
IMSE at GMI  (p1 of 3)
                        Welcome To The IMSE Home Page
                                     at
                    GMI Engineering & Management Institute


                       Page is constantly being updated.
          ____________________________________________________________
               [1]About Industrial & Maufacturing Engineering
                     [2]Undergraduate Catalog 1994 - 1995
               [3]Manufacturing Systems Engineering Curriculum
                     [4]Industrial Engineering Curriculum
-- press space for next page --
  Arrow keys: Up and Down to move. Right to follow a link; Left to go
back.
 H)elp O)ptions P)rint G)o M)ain screen Q)uit /=search [delete]=history
list
```

Chapter Summary

This chapter introduced what many people consider to be the Internet: the World Wide Web. The chapter looked at text and graphical browsers. A major portion of the chapter was devoted to the creation of HTML pages. The chapter concluded with a look at some of the newer innovations for the Web, VRML and JAVA.

Key Terms

Browsers
Home Pages
HTML
HTTP
Hypertext
Images
JAVA
Links
lynx
Tags
URL
VRML
Web Server
World Wide Web
WWW

Problems

1. Use your browser to point to *http://www.yahoo.com.* Print this page out.
2. Use any one of the search engines mentioned in the chapter. Search for stereo lithography. Print out the list of sites found.
3. Create an HTML page which has your name, your class and your instructor's name on it. Print out a copy of the page.
4. Modify the page created in Problem 4 so that you have a horizontal line above and below your name. Print out a copy of the page.
5. Create an HTML page which has some text elements formatted with the following attributes: bold, italics, heading 2, underlined and blockquotes. Print this page out.
6. Create an HTML page which has a bulleted list with the four seasons of the year on it. Print out this page.
7. Modify the HTML page created in Problem 6 so that each of the four bullets on the original list has a sublist of two items that you like about each season on it. Print out this page.
8. Create an HTML page that has your name on it. Insert any graphic image that you like (or one suggested by your instructor). Print out a copy of the page.
9. Create two separate HTML pages. Create a text link from one page to the other. Test the pages to ensure that the link works. Print out a copy of the two pages.
10. Modify one of the two text links in Problem 9 so that it is a graphic link. Print the two pages out.

CHAPTER

7

Live Communications on the Internet

SCIENCE/ENGINEERING SPOTLIGHT: BAR CODE TECHNOLOGIES

You probably don't give those little bars at the bottom of groceries much thought. How about the lines at the bottom of the address label on your mail? Have you seen the weird squares that look like a psychologist's ink-blot test? All of these items are bar codes. Bar codes are actually an amazing innovation in the tracking of packages. Bar codes no longer have to be one-dimensional like the UPC labels on food. Two-dimensional bar codes have been created that allow even more information to be stored in a small area. Bar codes allow efficient sorting of items to take place, accurately, at very high rates of speed and without much human intervention.

OBJECTIVES

With all of the other Internet services that we have looked at, we were looking at what people had written/posted/sent in the past. The Internet provides for live "real-time" communications just as well, though. We will examine the two main types of this communication service: Talk and IRC. The chapter will conclude in an examination of the future of real-time communications and the extensions that have been created for the World Wide Web.

7.1 TALK

Talk is a program that exists on many UNIX systems (it has other names on different computers such as DEC's VAX/VMS *phone* command). Talk simply tries to locate another user that you specify, and if that user is logged in, notify the user that you wish to talk to him/her. Talk is like a telephone conversation in that both parties can "speak" and "hear" simultaneously. Talk is completely text-based with each party appearing in their own screen window.

Let's look at a talk example where I try to talk to a user named *bjames*, who isn't logged in on my local system.

```
defiant{sjames}11% talk bjames
------------------------------------------------------------------------
[No connection yet]
[Your party is not logged on]


------------------------------------------------------------------------



------------------------------------------------------------------------
```

That didn't work, but user *dougj* is requesting to talk with me. I can answer him by typing `talk dougj@nova.gmi.edu`. You might notice that this user is not on the same system that I am on. He happens to be at GMI, but, he could be on the other side of the world using the Internet and I could still talk with him.

```
defiant{sjames}12%

Message from Talk_Daemon@defiant at 11:49 ...
talk: connection requested by dougj@nova.gmi.edu.
talk: respond with:  talk dougj@nova.gmi.edu

talk dougj@nova.gmi.edu
------------------------------------------------------------------------
[No connection yet]
[Connection established]
Yes?


------------------------------------------------------------------------
Just wanted to see what you were up to!
```

```
Talk with you later!

-----------------------------------------------------------------
```

My conversation appears in the lower window (what I type) and the other user's response appears in the upper window. When either person wants to quit the Talk facility, all they have to do is press *Control-C*.

This particular version of Talk will only let two people communicate at once. There are multiple-party talk versions such as *ntalk*, *otalk*, and *ytalk*, however. You might also want to try using the *finger* command to see if your party is logged in before wasting the time trying a Talk session.

7.2 IRC - INTERNET RELAY CHAT

IRC is the Internet equivalent of the chat rooms that are located on popular Bulletin Board Systems (BBS). The idea is that someone creates a chat room dedicated to a specific subject and people who are on-line can enter the chat room and join in on the conversation. That is the basic idea of IRC, except the folks who can enter the chat room are those with IRC access on the Internet.

You will find that IRC is much more chaotic to converse on than UseNet or e-mail. The reason for this is that the people who are on a given channel (IRC-speak for a chat room) are all communicating when they feel like it, so it's much more of a rambling conversation than the well-thought-out and posted messages on the other aforementioned Internet services.

The plus side of IRC is that it is free; there are no limits to the number or types of channels that are active, and there is no limit to the number of people who can participate at any given time.

Running IRC

To run IRC you must either locate an IRC client program to run on your computer or Telnet to an IRC provider. If you have an IRC program on your system and you need to locate an IRC server to use, here are a few addresses:

IRC SERVERS BY STATE:

irc.netsys.com	CA
irc.caltech.edu	CA
irc.indiana.edu	IN
csa.bu.edu	MA
wpu.wpi.edu	MA
irc.tc.umn.edu	MN
mothra.syr.edu	NY

If you just want to use Telnet to gain access to public IRC clients, here are some available hosts:

PUBLIC IRC CLIENTS:

wildcar.ecn.uoknor.edu 6667
vinson.ecn.uoknor.edu 6667
sci.dixie.edu 6667
bradenville.andrew.cmu.edu
santafe.santafe.edu login:*irc*

Using IRC

Once you have connected to your IRC site, you can start accessing different channels. You may first want to pick a nickname. If you don't pick one, your username will be used by default. Nicknames make IRC more personal and fun and accommodate those users who have meaningless numeric usernames.

If you do pick a nickname, here are a few tips:

- Stay with one nickname and don't change it
- Keep the nickname simple, without special characters
- Limit nicknames to nine characters in length

To set your nickname, type */NICK nickname_you_want.* Here's a sample of what an IRC screen looks like:

```
*** - 30/6/1996 21:19
*** - Welcome to the NetOne(tm) IRC Server
*** -
*** - Appropriate Language and Behavior are mandatory.
*** -
*** - User Bots are not allowed on Channel #NetOne.
*** -
*** - Report problems to Milkman (tlyon) or Lane (lane), your IRC Operator.
*** -
*** - Thanks for joining us, we're glad you're here.
*** -
*** End of /MOTD command.
*** Channel     Users  Topic
*** #other      1
*** #netone     3      Ahh, Sleep... Sleep is the only Adventure.
*** #cyberpsychos      2      Giant insects wearing plaid linoleum negliges
*** End of /LIST
*** sjames (sjames@defiant.gmi.edu) has joined channel #netone
*** Topic for #netone: Ahh, Sleep... Sleep is the only Adventure.
*** The topic was set by jeff 29732 sec ago
*** Users on #netone: sjames gutz @Ventrue_AFK @VCSBot
*** Channel #netone was created at Fri Aug  9 08:14:42 1996
 12:23PM [1] sjames #netone (M: 2)  ircII2.8.2-EPIC3 -- Type /help for help
>
```

The last line ">" is where you will type in all IRC commands.

How do you find what channels are available to join? Try the /LIST command. /LIST will show every channel that is available. This could be quite a large list.

All channels will start with a # sign. Even if someone is talking about a channel and doesn't provide the # sign, it needs to be there. This is how we separate the users from the channels.

To join a channel, just type /JOIN #channel. Once you've joined a channel, anything you type will appear to all users of the channel with your nickname in brackets. The bracketed nickname is used to let the other users of the channel know who typed what.

To leave a channel, type /LEAVE #channel or /PART #channel. Either one does the same thing.

There is IRC help available by typing /HELP or /HELP command. If I wanted to know what the /LIST command does, for example, I could type /HELP list.

To find out who is on a channel use the /WHO command. This will list the nicknames of all the people on the channel. For each user that is on the channel you will see a status value: A indicates that the user is Away from their machine at the moment, H indicates that the user is on their machine and active in IRC, * indicates that a person is an IRCop (an IRC operator) and @ indicates that the user is a ChanOp (channel operator).

If you need to leave IRC for a minute, you can inform other users with the /AWAY command. For example /AWAY I'll be back in a minute will appear on everyone else's screen. You will receive a reply letting you know that you were marked as away. To deactivate the away status just type /AWAY again.

The other user-related commands that provide information on channel users are /WHOIS which tells who is currently on the channel and /WHOWAS, which tells who was on the channel.

If you are annoyed by the messages that certain users are typing, you can ignore them via the /IGNORE command. The typical format of the /IGNORE command is /IGNORE *nickname option*. *Option* could be of ALL (ignore all messages from this user), NONE (ignore none of this user's messages), MSG (ignore only private messages sent with */MSG*), NOTICE (ignore only private messages sent with /NOTICE) and INVITE (ignores channel invites from the user). If you enter /IGNORE without the nickname or option, it will list all of the people you are ignoring and what option you have set for each.

Personal conversations can be carried out on any IRC channel. The /MSG command will allow you to send a message to one or more specific users. The format is /MSG *usernickname*$_1$*[,usernickname*$_2$*,usernickname*$_n$*] text*. The recipients of the message will see your nickname in asterisks to indicate that the message they just received is private versus the usual bracketed public messages. /NOTICE is a command that is identical in nature to /MSG except that hyphens are used in place of the asterisks.

If you want to send a fairly long private communication, you should use the /QUERY command which will allow you to type a long message. To start the /QUERY command type /QUERY *usernickname*. At this point you can enter your message. When you are finished type the /QUERY command by itself.

Sometimes you may wish to chat in private on IRC. If you want to send encrypted messages for security reasons, IRC provides some support. Let's say that users *sjames* and *dblasdell* agree to use *nova* for their password:

User *sjames* would type:

```
/ENCRYPT dblasdell nova
```

User *dblasdell* would type:

```
/ENCRYPT sjames nova
```

Now the messages between users *sjames* and *dblasdell* would be encrypted and only they would see the unencrypted message. Everyone else would receive a `<sjames> [ENCRYPTED MESSAGE]` notice.

OTHER MISCELLANEOUS IRC COMMANDS:

- If you want to review some past text, type the command `/LASTLOG` *lines_to_review*. If you want to view messages from only one user use the `/LASTLOG` *nickname [-Public] lines_to_review* command. If the *-Public* option is used, it shows only the messages sent from *nickname* to everyone on the channel.
- To create your own channel just type `/JOIN` *#newchannelname*. You might want to set the channel mode by `/MODE` **channel* or *nickname* +options*.

AVAILABLE CHANNEL OPTIONS:

`i`	Users must be invited to join
`l<number>`	Only a certain number of users can be on at once
`m`	Only people with operator privileges can talk
`n`	`/MSGs` from outside the channel are not allowed
`p`	The channel is private
`s`	The channel is secret (it doesn't show up in `/LIST` command)
`t`	Only channel operators can change the channel's topic

AVAILABLE USER OPTIONS:

`in`	Make yourself invisible
`o`	IRC-operator status
`s`	Allows you to receive server messages

One Final Note: IRCbots

IRCbots are automated programs set up by IRC users to perform certain tasks over IRC. IRCbots are often seen as wasteful and annoying, such as the Barneybot which sings the Barney theme song. Only a few servers will allow their use. IRCbots are simply programs that IRC users can interact with such as a joke bot, bartender bot, poetry bots and so forth.

7.3 FUTURE OF LIVE COMMUNICATIONS

If the thought of real-time text conversation has enchanted you, you will be pleasantly surprised to know that there are a few real-time voice programs available. One of the programs, InternetPhone, allow users of computers with audio capabilities to join an IRC channel and audibly talk over the Internet. You speak through your computer's microphone to other users across the world and you will hear their replies over the computer's speakers. This is as close as you can get to having free worldwide long distance phone calls, since you won't directly be picking up the tab.

Another audio facility, VoiceChat, just requires two multimedia computers using TCP/IP to talk to one another without having to resort to IRC.

RealAudio

If the thought of talking to someone real-time has interested you, how would you like the ability to listen to music, sports and talk shows real-time on your computer? RealAudio by Progressive Networks (*http://www.realaudio.com*) allows real-time transmissions of audio material to be sent over the Internet.

RealAudio is an add-in that is available to a number of browsers. Once you have a copy of RealAudio installed, point it at the following sites:

ABC RadioNet	http://www.abcradionet.com
C/Net Radio	http://www.cnet.com/Content/Radio/index.html
ESPN SportsZone	http://espnet.sportszone.com
National Public Radio	http://www.realaudio.com/contentp.npr

Here's what Progressive Networks, Inc's. RealAudio home page looks like (*see next page*):

StreamWorks

Audio is not the only item that is available on demand. Video feeds are available too. Xing Technologies' StreamWorks (*http://www.xingtech.com*) is a browser add-in that handles both audio and video feeds.

The following is a list of some Xing broadcasting sites:

Bloomberg News Radio	http://www.bloomberg.com/cgi-bin/tdisp.sh?wbbr/index.html	audio/video
iRock Radio	http://www.irock.com	audio
KMPS, Seattle	http://www.kmps.com	audio
KPIG, Santa Cruz	http://www.kpig.com	audio
KZOK, Seattle	http://www.kzok.com	audio
NBC Pro Financial Network	http://www.xingtech.com/nbc.html	video

Here's Xing Technologies' Corporation home page:

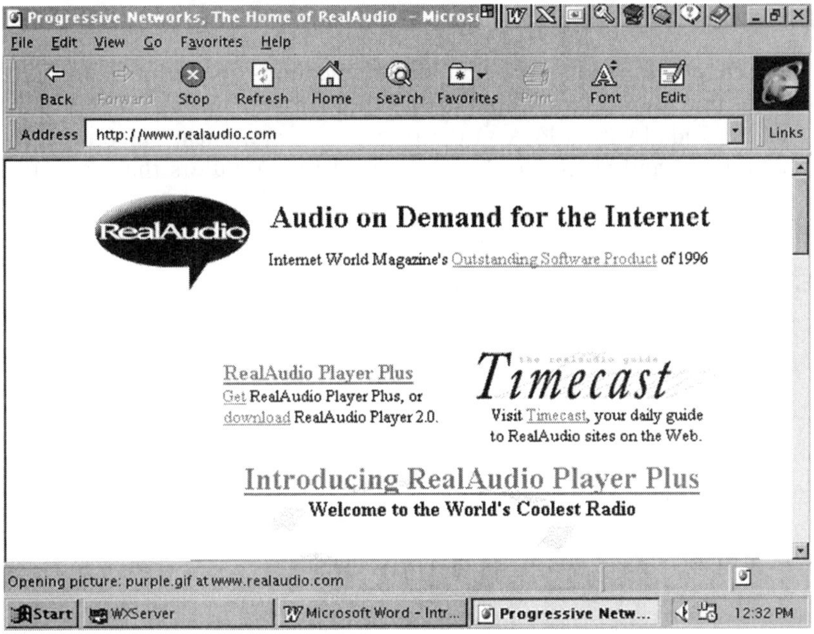
Progressive Networks, The Home of RealAudio - Micros
File Edit View Go Favorites Help
Back Forward Stop Refresh Home Search Favorites Print Font Edit
Address http://www.realaudio.com
Links
RealAudio
Audio on Demand for the Internet
Internet World Magazine's Outstanding Software Product of 1996
RealAudio Player Plus
Get RealAudio Player Plus, or
download RealAudio Player 2.0.
Timecast
Visit Timecast, your daily guide
to RealAudio sites on the Web.
Introducing RealAudio Player Plus
Welcome to the World's Coolest Radio
Opening picture: purple.gif at www.realaudio.com
Start WXServer Microsoft Word - Intr... Progressive Netw... 12:32 PM

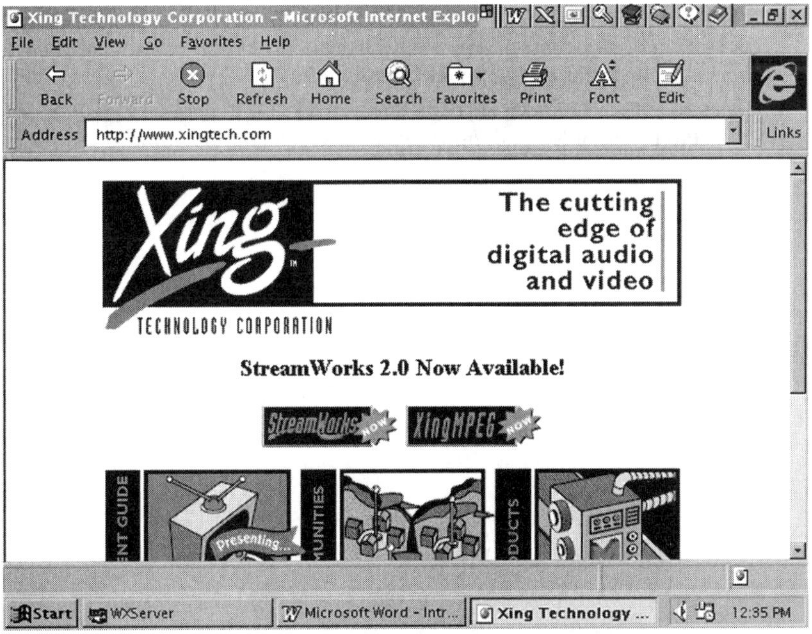
Xing Technology Corporation - Microsoft Internet Explo
File Edit View Go Favorites Help
Back Forward Stop Refresh Home Search Favorites Print Font Edit
Address http://www.xingtech.com
Links
Xing
TECHNOLOGY CORPORATION
The cutting
edge of
digital audio
and video
StreamWorks 2.0 Now Available!
StreamWorks
XingMPEG
Start WXServer Microsoft Word - Intr... Xing Technology ... 12:35 PM

Chapter Summary

This chapter looked at real-time communications on the Internet. Two text-based programs that allow users to chat to one another were examined: talk and IRC. The chapter concluded with a look at the future of communications on the Internet, in which both audio and video can be transferred to computers that are equipped to receive such transmissions.

Key Terms

Channel
IRC
IRCbots
IRCop
Nicknames
RealAudio
StreamWorks
Talk

Problems

1. Determine if your institution has a "talk" or "phone" command. If it does, try conversing with a friend.
2. Access IRC and join a group or two. Write up a summary of your impression of IRC.
3. Determine if your browser supports RealAudio. If it does, listen to and report on the top stories from ABC RadioNet *http://www.abcradionet.com*.
4. Determine if your browser supports StreamWorks. If it does, check out what's happening on the NBC Pro Financial Network *http://www.xingtech.com/nbc.html*.

CHAPTER

8

Computer Security and the Internet

SCIENCE/ENGINEERING SPOTLIGHT: N/C MACHINING AND CAM

N/C machining, or numerical control machining, is the automated direction of a tool to do some task through numerical data and instructions. The idea for N/C came about from the manufacture of helicopter blades. At the time, circa World War II, helicopter blades were made by hand, and were at best a trial-and-error process. N/C got its birth when it was realized that if several data points on a good blade were sampled, another decent blade could be machined by a small group of people working together. One individual would call off x and y coordinate cutting information and a couple of other folks would actually turn the machine to the given coordinates. With the advent of computers, this whole process would continue to get more precise and repeatable.

Computer Aided Manufacturing allows a computer user to generate the geometry of a part on a computer screen. The user can then simulate the machining process on the computer screen, and if everything looks correct, the computer user can then convert the geometry information into N/C machining data. Once the N/C data has been created, the user can then send the information to the appropriate machine, insert a workpiece and watch as the machine creates the part. The marriage of N/C machining and Computer Aided Manufacturing has led to quick turnaround times in creating prototypes of parts and has helped reduce costly errors of misprogrammed N/C instructions through the simulation of the cutting path on the computer screen.

OBJECTIVES

Who has to worry about security on the Internet? If you are an Internet user, then you should worry. This isn't to say that you need to take a paranoid stance and never use the Internet. Instead, you should just be aware of the dangers and take the appropriate measures to keep yourself as secure as possible. We are going to examine each of the potential threats on the Internet and look into means of protecting ourselves from the threat. This chapter will examine password attacks.

8.1 PASSWORD ATTACKS

The most common way that a cracker gets into a computer system is by gaining access to someone's password. Many computer users have horrendous password habits: poorly chosen passwords, no password or the password is posted next to the computer on a sticky note adhered to the monitor. The truth of the matter is that once a cracker has access to your account, that individual effectively becomes you and has access to whatever you have access to.

You may think that you are safe on the Internet though since you have set a good password. After all, how would a cracker even know your username. Remember our friend the *Finger* command? *Finger* legitimately provides information about a user, including their username. Now the cracker has one half of the requirements to access the system; all that remains is getting the right password.

Many sites that are new on the Internet were created by designers who didn't realize all the holes that were in the operating system they were using. It is possible with some systems to get a copy of the encrypted password file. Once a person has the encrypted password file, all that person needs to do is grab a copy of the publicly available *crack* program and some dictionaries. *Crack* will take each word in the dictionary, encrypt many variations of it and see if it matches the password. It is not unusual to gain 10 - 15% of all passwords from a site using *crack*. The time required to crack an average password file is only a couple of hours.

How do you protect yourself? Here's the password checklist:

- Make sure the password is not publicly displayed.
- Make sure you use a password and change that password every so often.

- Use a password that is not related to you and cannot be looked up in any dictionary.
- Use letters, numbers and punctuation in the password (mixed-case if possible).
- The password should at least be 6 characters long.
- Think of implementing one-time passwords.
- Don't use the same password on every system you have access to.
- If your computer comes with a boot password, use it.
- Get rid of passwords and implement some kind of a physical hardware passkey system.

8.2 SOCIAL ENGINEERING

Social engineering is a type of attack in which a cracker attempts to gain access to a system by impersonating someone within an organization (another valid user, someone in the information systems department, a hired consultant, etc.). A typical social engineering attack will occur in the form of someone calling as a system administrator who needs to log on in your name to check some system parameter (access capabilities, response time, etc.). These con-jobs are carried out so gracefully that most organizations don't even know they've been hit.

Social engineering attacks primarily occur in one of two ways:

- Telephone Calls
- In-Person Visits—Crackers have been known to rummage through trash cans looking for "in's"; some have been bold enough to come in to an organization claiming they have been hired as outside consultants.

How to protect yourself from social engineering scams:

- Never give your password to anyone over the phone; and don't readily distribute it to people who show up in person.
- Don't leave yourself logged in while you're away from your computer.
- If you don't recognize personnel who claim to be with your organization that need to work with you and/or your computer, ask for their company I.D. card or some other form of identification.
- If the person claims that he or she has been contracted as a consultant, verify this with someone you know in your organization.

8.3 DATA INTERCEPTION

Data interception includes many different areas: capturing someone's username and password; gaining access to important private company data; or logging the activities carried out on a particular machine. Let's examine the common ways that crackers carry out this type of security breach.

Packet Sniffers

Packet sniffers capture the actual data that is being transmitted over the physical media connecting computers. These media could be wires, fiber optics, microwave, etc. The basic idea is to target an address or group of addresses and copy every packet to a file. This file can be later examined for the information that was being transmitted. The main advantage to this security breach is that it can be carried out with almost no means of detection; and since all data must be transmitted between machines, a cracker has access to just about everything, even on computers that are considered to be "secure."

A slight twist on the sniffer angle is IP spoofing, in which you forge packets such that your computer will appear to belong on a given network or system; hence you again gain access to packets which you should not have.

How to protect yourself from packet sniffing:

- There are implementations of software packages called *packet wrappers* which essentially encrypt the original data packet at the source, put a wrapper around it with the source and destination address and then transmit the encrypted packet to the destination computer. The destination computer then must unwrap the packet with the correct key and the data becomes useable. While this doesn't prevent a cracker from packet sniffing, it will not directly allow the cracker access to the original data. If a sufficient encryption package is used, this will effectively limit what the cracker can gain from this type of security hole.
- If you can't put a packet wrapper on, then at least think about encrypting your data before sending it. Some of the available packages include *DES* (Data Encryption Standard), *RSA* (Rivest, Shamir and Adleman) and *PGP* (Pretty Good Privacy), which has been mentioned before.

Keystroke Logging

Keystroke logging is just what it sounds like, someone is gathering all of the keys that are pressed on a particular computer. The logging may occur from a program that has been modified to send the keystroke to its original destination as well as to a file; another alternative is to monitor the electromagnetic radiation being emitted from the computer. While this sounds kind of *Star Trek*-ish, it can and has been done. Since most keyboard controllers communicate in the 15 - 25 Mhz range and the video controller is in the 40 - 50 Mhz range according to FCC standards, anyone can purchase a radio receiver and an oscilloscope to spy on the computer.

How to protect yourself:

- If your worry is the logging program, read the next section. If it's the electromagnetic radiation approach that has you worried, put up the appropriate shielding or purchase a TEMPEST machine. TEMPEST machines meet government and military security standards to avoid having their EMR signatures read.

Modified Programs

There's nothing more difficult to detect than a modified program. Think of what could (and does) happen if an individual had the source to your operating system's login program. The individual could modify the code in such a way that it would echo your login id and password attempt to a file, but still pass that information on to the original part of the login program so that nothing has apparently changed to you. The modifier of the program could then periodically grab a copy of that file and would have access to most (if not all) accounts. Worse yet, there are utilities that allow you to change the file size, date and time to match the original, so nothing seems out of place.

How to protect yourself:

- You should take "snapshots" of the system periodically, recording the original file date and size. While there are utilities that can permit a cracker to modify this information, it provides a little bit more peace of mind. If the number of files in the snapshot is greatly increasing or decreasing, there is a possibility that some kind of a security breach has occurred.
- You may also want to get a package that computes checksums on the files on your computer. A checksum is nothing more than a number which is arrived at by subjecting a file to a mathematical algorithm. Once the checksum has been computed, modifying the date and time to hide the changed program will not be enough. If the "insides" of the program have changed, the checksum will not match against the original and will be flagged by the security program. Remember, though, for every security hole plugged, another is invented. There are software packages available which will generate a new checksum for the modified program and place that size in the checksum database hiding the discovery of the modified program.

8.4 OPERATING SYSTEM/PROTOCOL HOLES

Let's face it, with the complex state of today's operating systems, people are bound to make mistakes when developing the programs that make them up. Unfortunately crackers have nothing better to do than to try to find and exploit these holes. The only safe operating system today is one which is on the computer that is never turned on!

How to protect yourself:

- Many people think that when they delete a file it is gone. In MS-DOS there is a program called *undelete* which will restore deleted files. Some vendors provide packages which will write a series of all 1s and then all 0s over the original file before it is deleted. This way if an individual undeletes the file, it will be junk.
- Make sure that you have assigned the proper file permissions to your files. Operating systems such as Unix will allow the owner of a file to determine who can access a file and what type of access they have to it. You should investigate this area of your O.S.

- Keep up-to-date on patches that are available from the operating system vendor. Apply the patches and upgrades as soon as possible. Read any newsgroups dealing with your computer/operating system/protocol so that you are as aware as possible of holes that have been located.
- Implement a firewall to protect your host. A firewall is a dedicated computer that you program to allow certain services and addresses in and out of your network. Most firewalls allow you to deny ranges of addresses, protocols, ports and services.

8.5 COMPUTER VIRUSES

Computer viruses are programs which have the ability to reproduce and spread across a computer system and/or network. The program may contain specific instructions which will perform a destructive task if a given event occurs. Viruses typically attack executable programs and diskette boot sectors, however any piece of data which might be read into the computer's memory and executed is a possible source for transporting a virus. Even something an innocuous as Microsoft Word's Macro function has been used. Viruses can attack hardware, software and data, meaning that they are bad news and can do lots of damage.

HOW DO YOU GET VIRUSES?

- A program is executed from an infected disk
- A user attempts to boot from an infected disk
- An infected program is downloaded and executed
- An infected program is transferred over a computer network and executed
- An infected program is specifically planted in a target computer system where it will be executed.

WHAT ARE SOME OF THE INDICATIONS OF AN INFECTION?

- Access lights turn on for devices which are not being used
- Changes in a file's size, date or time
- Computers unexpectedly start rebooting
- Disk access seems excessive for simple tasks
- Disk space is suddenly reduced
- Files suddenly start vanishing
- Keyboard keys do odd things or lock up
- More marked bad spots appear on hard drives
- New files suddenly appear
- Programs attempt to write to write-protected disks
- Programs take longer to load or run slower than usual
- Strange noise or music is played over the speaker
- The amount of available memory is decreased

- The system can no longer properly boot up
- There are unexplained hidden files present
- Unusual displays or error messages appear

Any and all of these events can be explained by legitimate programs. However many of these events together or repeated occurrences of several may signal viral trouble.

PROGRAMS SIMILAR TO VIRUSES:

- Trojan Horse: A program designed to look like a valid application, such as a spreadsheet or word processor. When the user is running the Trojan Horse, a destructive task is typically occurring. For example the user may believe he or she is saving data to a disk when in fact the hard drive is being formatted. A Trojan Horse cannot reproduce itself.
- Logic Bomb: A set of instructions which will activate if some given conditions are met. For example if a user is running a program to produce payroll checks and employee #953 is missing, erase all of the payroll data files.
- Worm: A usually benign program which spreads itself through networks. Worms usually spread through security holes in the computer's operating system and may tie up system resources until they are removed.

HOW TO PROTECT YOURSELF:

- Avoid booting the computer from floppy disks
- Backup all original software and install only from the backup disks
- Backup your computer system often
- Limit software being brought in from home
- Never use bootlegged, hacked or pirated software even for evaluation purposes
- Purchase name brand software and insist on shrinkwrapped packages only
- Use virus scanners often and update the scanners frequently

8.6 WHAT TO DO IF YOU ARE ATTACKED

If you know that you have been attacked, you may want to run through the following list. It's quite possible, though, that you may have been attacked and not realize it for quite a while, if ever.

WHAT TO DO IF YOU DISCOVER A SECURITY BREACH:

- Disconnect from the Internet and perform some housecleaning. You might have to reload your system from backups or from scratch.
- Force every user to change their password.
- You may want to contact CERT, the Computer Emergency Response Team at Carnegie-Mellon University. They may not be able to help you out of your trouble, but they will at least see if the attack is similar to other current attacks. CERT publishes security advisories, so your misery may help others avoid it.

Chapter Summary

This chapter examined some of the basic security issues concerning computer use and the Internet. The most commonly exploited security breach is the use of pirated passwords. The chapter presented some suggestions on creating "good" passwords. The chapter also examined other ways in which computer systems can be violated: social engineering, data interception and operating system/protocol holes. Computer viruses, a continuing threat to Internet users, were briefly studied and suggestions on ways to ward off virus attacks were presented. The chapter concluded with a look at what to do if a system breach is discovered.

Key Terms

Checksums
Crack
Data Interception
Infection
IP Spoofing
Keypress Logging
Logic Bombs
Modified Programs
Operating System Holes
Packet Sniffers
Password Attacks
Patches
Protocol Holes
Social Engineering
System Snapshots
TEMPEST
Trojan Horse
Virus
Worm

Bibliography

CHESWICK, WILLIAM & STEVEN BELLOVIN. *Firewalls & Internet Security*. Reading, MA:Addison-Wesley, 1994.

DOUGHERTY, DALE & RICHARD KONAN. *The Mosaic Handbook*. Sebastopol, CA:O'Reilly & Associates, 1994.

FRASSE, MICHAEL. *The Windows Internet Tour Guide*. Ventana Press, 1994.

HAHN, HARLEY & RICK STOUT. *The Internet Complete Reference*. Berkeley, CA:Osborne, 1994.

HAHN, HARLEY & RICK STOUT. *Internet Yellow Pages, 2nd edition*. Berkeley, CA:Osborne, 1995.

HORTON, WILLIAM, LEE TAYLOR, ARTHUR IGNACIO, & NANCY HOFT. *The Web Page Design Cookbook*. New York, NY:John Wiley & Sons, 1996.

JAMES, SCOTT. *Computer Virus Seminar*. 1990.

JAMES, SCOTT. *Information System Security Seminar*. 1992.

KARPINSKI, RICHARD. *Beyond HTML*. Berkeley, CA:Osborne, 1996.

KEHOE, BRENDAN. *Zen and the Art of the Internet*. Englewood Cliffs, NJ:Prentice Hall, 1996.

NORTHWESTNET. *Internet Passport, 5th edition*. Englewood Cliffs, NJ:Prentice Hall, 1995.

O'REILLY & ASSOCIATES. *Unix in a Nutshell System V Edition*. Sebastopol, CA:O'Reilly & Associates, 1992.

QUE BOOKS. *Using the Internet, 2nd edition*. Indianapolis, IN:Que, 1995.

QUE BOOKS. *Using UNIX*. Indianapolis, IN:Que, 1990.

Trademark Information

Apple, Macintosh, & Mac are trademarks of Apple Computer, Inc.

CompuServe is a trademark of CompuServe, Inc.

DEC, VAX, VMS & VT100 are registered trademarks of Digital Equipment Corporation

Ethernet is a registered trademark of Xerox Corporation

Fido and Fidonet are trademarks of Tom Jennings

Hewlett-Packard is a trademark of Hewlett-Packard Corporation

IBM & IBM-PC are registered trademarks of International Business Machines Corporation

Java, NFS, SUN & SUNOS are trademarks of Sun Microsystems, Inc.

Knowbot is a trademark of the Corporation for National Research Institute

Microsoft, Windows, MS-DOS, Word & Excel are trademarks of Microsoft Corporation

Pine is a trademark of the University of Washington

Quicktime is a registered trademark of Apple Computer, Inc.

RealAudio is a trademark of Progressive Networks

StreamWorks is a trademark of Xing Technologies

UNIX is a registered trademark of AT&T Bell Laboratories

APPENDIX

A

The TCP/IP Protocol

In this Appendix, we will take a little closer look at TCP/IP and its components. Here we will examine the buzzwords that you will encounter when reading many Internet documents. You don't need to know any of this information to use the Internet, however, if you will be setting up applications on your computer, some of these issues might come up, so this section serves as a quick reference to the world of TCP/IP.

Protocols

Transport Protocols: Control the movement of data between two computers.

TCP (Transmission Control Protocol) is a connection-based service between two machines that are connected and in communication with each other at all times.

UDP (User Datagram Protocol) is a connectionless service meaning that data can be sent and received between machines that are not currently connected or communicating with each other.

Routing Protocols: Handle the addressing of the data and determine the best way to get the data to its destination. Routing protocols are also responsible for breaking up large messages and reassembling those messages at their destination.

IP (Internet Protocol) is responsible for the actual transmission of data.

ICMP (Internet Control Message Protocol) handles status messages for IP, such as errors and changes that affect the routing of information.

RIP (Routing Information Protocol) is one of several protocols that determine the best routing method to deliver a message.

OSPF (Open Shortest Path First) is an alternative protocol for determining routing.

Network Addresses: These related protocols are used for associating IP addresses and hostnames.

ARP (Address Resolution Protocol) determines the unique [Ethernet] numeric address of machines on the network from the machine's IP address.
DNS (Domain Name Service) determines numeric addresses from machine names.
RARP (Reverse Address Resolution Protocol) determines addresses of machines, but in reverse of ARP.

User Services: These are applications that a user can run.

BOOTP (Boot Protocol) starts up a network machine by getting information from a server such as what the machine's IP Address should be and so on.
FTP (File Transfer Protocol) transfers files between machines.
TELNET allows remote logins to other machines.

Gateway Protocols: These help the network communicate routing and status information.

EGP (Exterior Gateway Protocol) transfers external network routing information.
GGP (Gateway to Gateway Protocol) transfers gateway routing information.
IGP (Internal Gateway Protocol) transfers internal network routing information.

Miscellaneous Protocols:

NFS (Network File System) permits the sharing of directories and disks across a network. This means that directories on a remote computer can be accessed just as if they were local directories.
NIS (Network Information Service) allows user account information such as passwords and logins to be shared across a network, cutting down on the amount of maintenance that needs to be performed.
RPC (Remote Procedure Call) allows remote applications to communicate with each other in a simple, efficient manner.
SMTP (Simple Mail Transport Protocol) transfers mail between computers.
SNMP (Simple Network Management Protocol) is a service that sends status messages about the network and devices connected to it.

Internet Address Classes

When an entity gets assigned an IP Address it will be one of three possible classes:

Class A - Starts with a number between 0 - 127
Class B - Starts with a number between 128 - 191
Class C - Starts with a number between 192 and 223

The primary difference between the address classes is the number of computers which can be put on that type of network. For example, a class C address will have the first three triplets assigned, meaning that you can assign the last triplet for each computer that needs to be connected (roughly 255 machines). A class B address assigns the first two triplets, leaving around 65,000 numbers that can be assigned to an organization's computers. Finally, a class A address assigns the first triplet, leaving about 16,000,000 numbers that can be assigned.

Submasks: Many times software wants to know what submask to use. Think of this as a question of how many machines are within an organization's class. A 0 indicates all, so if you need a Class C submask, use 255.255.255.0; for a Class B network, use 255.255.0.0 as the submask; and for a Class A network, use 255.0.0.0.

APPENDIX B

Miscellaneous Internet Programs

This Appendix takes a look at some other programs that are somewhat useful when working with the Internet. These programs were not included in the main section of the text since not all computer systems have versions of these programs available.

IP Address Resolver

Sometimes it is convenient to know the IP address associated with some hostname. Fortunately there is an IP address resolver that is available via e-mail. To use this service send e-mail to *resolve@cs.widener.edu* with site *hostname* as the message body. You will receive a reply which shows the hostname's IP address.

There are also several programs around which perform the same task. One of the more popular is *nslookup*.

Here's an example of using *nslookup* where I find out the IP address to one of my computers called *defiant:*

```
nova{sjames}21% nslookup defiant.gmi.edu

Name:     defiant.gmi.edu
Address:  192.138.137.53
```

Ping

Ping is a program that is usually supplied with most TCP/IP packages that provides you with a means of determining whether or not a given computer is accessible from your location. Pinging is derived from the sound that a sonar echo makes underwater. If you have ping, you can enter a machine name or IP address following the ping command. If the remote machine is accessible, ping will provide you with some network statistics.

Let's trying pinging *nova* to see if it's "alive."

```
defiant:~$ ping nova.gmi.edu
PING nova.gmi.edu (192.138.137.2): 56 data bytes
64 bytes from 192.138.137.2: icmp_seq=0 ttl=255 time=1.7 ms
64 bytes from 192.138.137.2: icmp_seq=1 ttl=255 time=1.7 ms
64 bytes from 192.138.137.2: icmp_seq=2 ttl=255 time=1.6 ms
64 bytes from 192.138.137.2: icmp_seq=3 ttl=255 time=1.6 ms
64 bytes from 192.138.137.2: icmp_seq=4 ttl=255 time=1.7 ms
64 bytes from 192.138.137.2: icmp_seq=5 ttl=255 time=1.6 ms
64 bytes from 192.138.137.2: icmp_seq=6 ttl=255 time=1.7 ms
64 bytes from 192.138.137.2: icmp_seq=7 ttl=255 time=1.7 ms
64 bytes from 192.138.137.2: icmp_seq=8 ttl=255 time=1.7 ms
64 bytes from 192.138.137.2: icmp_seq=9 ttl=255 time=1.6 ms
64 bytes from 192.138.137.2: icmp_seq=10 ttl=255 time=1.6 ms
64 bytes from 192.138.137.2: icmp_seq=11 ttl=255 time=1.7 ms
64 bytes from 192.138.137.2: icmp_seq=12 ttl=255 time=2.0 ms

--- nova.gmi.edu ping statistics ---
13 packets transmitted, 13 packets received, 0% packet loss
round-trip min/avg/max = 1.6/1.6/2.0 ms
```

From the output that we received, we can see that *nova* is alive and that each packet that was sent to the computer was successfully received.

Traceroute

Traceroute shows you the path taken from your computer to some remote computer. This is more informational in nature than it is useful. However it is interesting to see just how you get to a foreign country or some faraway location. Another use is when the network is slow: traceroute may indicate that an alternative route is being taken due to one of the normal host computers being down.

Let's look at how we get to a computer in Australia from my location in Flint:

```
defiant:~$ traceroute monu6.cc.monash.edu.au
traceroute to monu6.cc.monash.edu.au (130.194.1.106), 30 hops max, 40 byte packets
 1  michnetrouter (192.138.137.1)  3.322 ms  3.85 ms  3.215 ms
 2  ser5.gfec.mich.net (198.110.9.9)  40.089 ms  58.899 ms  29.742 ms
 3  ser3.flint.mich.net (198.110.9.17)  72.361 ms  61.014 ms  80.031 ms
 4  198.111.116.17 (198.111.116.17)  142.633 ms  255.507 ms  205.273 ms
 5  cpe2-fddi-1.Chicago.mci.net (192.203.195.5)  176.323 ms  153.807 ms  139.514 ms
 6  borderx2-hssi2-0.WillowSprings.mci.net (204.70.104.117)  81.704 ms  132.908 ms
205.77 ms
 7  core2-fddi-1.WillowSprings.mci.net (204.70.104.65)  216.199 ms  106.716 ms
 8  * core1.SanFrancisco.mci.net (204.70.4.169)  194.972 ms  147.921 ms
 9  border2-fddi0-0.SanFrancisco.mci.net (204.70.3.162)  159.617 ms  127.378 ms
225.566 ms
10  telstra-ds3.SanFrancisco.mci.net (204.70.33.10)  154.796 ms  167.393 ms  283.497
ms
```

```
11  telstra.SanFrancisco.mci.net (204.70.204.6)  388.338 ms  413.46 ms  373.389 ms
12  Fddi0-0.pad-core1.Sydney.telstra.net (139.130.249.226)  344.235 ms  354.992 ms
387.793 ms
13  Hssi6-0.lon-core1.Melbourne.telstra.net (139.130.249.214)  334.611 ms  356.22 ms
452.099 ms
14  vic.gw.au (139.130.239.228)  341.471 ms  406.131 ms  350.333 ms
15  national.gw.au (139.130.239.54)  354.105 ms *  444.048 ms
16  vic-gw.vrn.EDU.AU (203.21.131.114)  309.91 ms  372.842 ms  2073.72 ms
17  nis-west-gw.vrn.EDU.AU (203.21.131.6)  635.058 ms  360.201 ms  333.168 ms
18  nis-east-gw.vrn.EDU.AU (203.21.131.46)  317.949 ms  553.96 ms  2468.91 ms
19  * monash-gw.vrn.EDU.AU (203.21.131.98)  304.465 ms  514.126 ms
20  clayton-gw.monash.edu.au (130.194.14.254)  545.008 ms  304.881 ms  403.691 ms
```

You can see that we went from Flint, through Chicago, Willow Springs, San Francisco, Sydney and Melbourne on our way to our destination.

APPENDIX

C

Common Internet Items

The following is a list of some of the common documents and objects that are often mentioned when you read about the Internet. This list provides you with the site and directory from which you can FTP the information.

ITEM	SITE	DIRECTORY
FYIs	*ftp.nisc.sri.com*	*fyi/fyi-index.txt*
Gold in Networks!	*ftp.nisc.sri.com*	*rfc/rfc1290.txt*
Gopher	*boombox.micro.umn.edu*	*pub/gopher/*
Hitchhiker's Guide	*ftp.nisc.sri.com*	*rfc/rfc1118.txt*
Internet Resource Guide	*nnsc.nsf.net*	*resource-guide/*
InterNIC Resources	*ds.internic.net*	*/rfc /fyi /std*
List of FTP Sites	*pilot.njin.net*	*pub/ftp-list/*
List of Whois Servers	*sipb.mit.edu*	*pub/whois/whois-servers.list*
Network Reading List	*ftp.uu.net*	*inet/doc/*
New User's Questions	*ftp.nisc.sri.com*	*fyi/fyi4.txt*
Public Access UNIX	*gvl.unisys.com*	*pub/nixpub/long*
RFCs	*ftp.nisc.sri.com*	*rfc/rfc-index.txt*
WAIS Information	*think.com*	*wais/*
Whois Registration	*nic.ddn.mil*	*netinfo/user-template.txt*
WWW	*info.cern.ch*	*pub/www/doc/the_www_book*
Yanoff Services List	*csd4.csd.uwm.edu*	*pub/inet.services.txt*
Zen & Art of Internet	*ftp.cs.widener.edu*	*pub/zen/*

Index

E

F

G

H

I

P

R

S

T

U

V

W

Y

Z